Rawsome Superfoods

Rawsome Superfoods

100+ Nutrient-Packed Recipes

Using Nature's Hidden Power to Help You Feel Your Best

Emily von Euw

bestselling author of *Rawsome Vegan Baking*,
creator of This Rawsome Vegan Life

PAGE STREET
PUBLISHING CO.

THIS BOOK IS FOR YOU, BABE.

PAGE STREET
PUBLISHING CO.

First published in 2018 by
Page Street Publishing Co.
27 Congress Street, Suite 105
Salem, MA 01970
www.pagestreetpublishing.com

Distributed by Macmillan, sales in Canada by The Canadian Manda Group.

22 21 20 19 18   1 2 3 4 5

ISBN-13: 978-1-62414-627-5
ISBN-10: 1-62414-627-9

Library of Congress Control Number: 2018943554

Cover design by Sara Pollard and book design by Meg Baskis for Page Street Publishing Co.
Photography by Emily von Euw

Printed and bound in China

CONTENTS

BASIC RECIPES, SAUCES & SYRUPS 205

INTRODUCTION

Greetings to you, new friend. My name is Emily von Euw, but you can call me Em. Let me introduce myself so you can learn a li'l bit about who wrote this book. At the moment, I'm 24 years old and attempting to live my best life (whatever that means). I identify as a nonbinary, genderqueer person and use they/them pronouns. I was born and raised in the lower mainland of British Columbia, Canada. This part of the world is known by its traditional, sovereign inhabitants—specifically the Coast Salish Nations—as Turtle Island, among other names. I am grateful to be a guest here. This cookbook is my guide to a concept of wellness that nurtures the body, mind, heart and spirit . . . they are connected, after all, and make up what we might call "me" or "you." In the following pages I share over 100 recipes to fuel our cells *and* selves, as well as philosophies about what wellness and health mean to me. Take what you will, since by no means do I ever desire to prescribe lessons to others. You know what is best for you, so trust that! We are all on our own path, yet these trails inevitably intersect. So if we can pick up dew drops of inspiration from others in this expansive, vibrant field of green life, I think that's beautiful and valuable.

I have always been a deeply passionate soul, finding reasons to live in both the micro and macro textures of this existence: from the color of moss on a mother log to the sound of my breath at the top of a mountain; from the sensual smell of sesame oil to the knowledge that food is both fuel and pleasure; and from the affectionate touch of a friend to the comfort I feel knowing there are multiple global communities of which I am a part, all working to better this earth while we are here and able. Veganism is one of those communities, as is feminism.

I aim to recognize intersections of identities to more fully understand—or at least have awareness—that as human beings, we are all coming from radically different places, yet have so much in common with one another. I am very thankful that I have found myself in the place I am now—my days are filled with nourishing foods, supportive relationships, lots of self care, music, writing, cooking and dancing. Every day is a gift, and I put effort into appreciating each one. Having said that, there are days when I am not able to exercise that labor.

I struggle with generalized anxiety disorder and depression, as well as other mental health issues involving disordered eating, gender dysphoria and obsessive and compulsive behaviors. Discovering the language to describe these experiences has been relieving and liberating, and simultaneously made their presence impossible to ignore or deny. Over the past few years, I have dedicated much time and energy into reflecting on my mental health, emotional well-being and personal boundaries as well as developing myriad coping mechanisms to keep my best self above water and thriving (or, on many days, at least surviving)!

Through personal experience and with the help of scientifically-researched data, I have learned a number of lifestyle habits that vastly improve my mood, energy levels, motivation and outlook on life. One huge piece is making sure that I drink enough water and eat enough nutritionally dense foods every week: the recipes in this book are perfectly compatible with this goal, but diet is just one part of wellness. Other helpful habits include meditation, yoga, creative outlets (like journaling, drawing, writing songs or poetry and appreciating other people's art), balancing alone time and social time, busy times and resting, and challenging myself as well as being kind to myself when I'm not up for a challenge. I practice radical self-love, which means that I aim to be as kind to myself as I am to others. So often I find I'm comparing myself to others in terms of success, "attractiveness," popularity and the like; this doesn't serve me and in fact only exacerbates my anxiety. Radical self-love, and self- and body-acceptance have taught me there is no need to be my own enemy. I list resources related to this on page 275.

We all deserve to be well and live a life which brings joy, safety and comfort.

This cookbook focuses on utilizing the power of food—the most nutrient-dense plant foods, to be specific—to protect, heal and nourish our bodies and spirits so we can be our best (however that looks)! Backed by scientific research and thousands of years of creative and informed usage in cultures around the world, it is clear there is a large collection of foods that have the ability to significantly and positively impact our well-being. Some of the foods you might already know, like broccoli, black beans and walnuts. Others could be new to you, such as ashwagandha, spirulina or camu camu. Regardless of where you're coming from with your awareness of these foods, they have proven, for many, to have life-changing effects on energy, longevity, immunity and wellness. I personally value mood-boosting adaptogens, anti-inflammatory spices and fiber-rich greens most of all. I believe it is important to share lessons once we learn them. Thus I felt compelled to center this cookbook around the power of my favorite ingredients, because they have uplifted me in my own life. In this book, compared to my previous works, I focus more intently on the researched benefits these ingredients can provide to our physical, emotional and mental health. I strongly believe in intuitive eating and living as a practice centered on self-compassion and self-love. So, please, recognize that you and your body know what is best for you. If that happens to be eating foods and recipes like the ones in this book, I am honored to be a part of that. If you only like a few recipes or concepts in here, that's okay too! Trust in yourself.

HOW TO USE THIS BOOK

DO WHAT WORKS FOR YOU

I speak from experience when I say food has the power to uplift my mood, instilling energy, motivation and gratitude to my days. Of course, the foods we eat and how we feel about those foods are equally important facets of eating. I do not believe in prescribing moral values to foods. There are no "good" or "bad" foods. Eating "healthy" doesn't necessarily mean eating the most nutritious foods all the time. If eating broccoli as a meal makes you feel bummed out or restricted, but eating an ice cream shake would bring you joy, then it sounds like the shake is the healthier option in this case, because mental health and happiness matter at least as much as physical health. Food is more than mere nutrition: it's about respecting ourselves enough to provide our bodies with what we need and deserve. Yes, consuming adequate vitamins, minerals and nutrients is important for optimizing physical health, improving mental outlook and preventing disease. But food is also about culture, politics, history, identity, pleasure and more. So find the balance that is right for you. Take care of yourself before anything else! More resources about this on page 275.

My recipes are meant to be simple, elegant ideas that inspire, so don't worry about following them exactly: make them yours! Consider the recipes as guidelines or jumping-off points for your own delicious, personalized versions. If you wanna switch out an ingredient or try a different technique, go for it. I deeply value creativity and improvisation in the kitchen (or wherever you make your meals), and certainly don't wanna hinder anyone else's.

That being said, I have tested all these recipes multiple times to make 'em just right. So in case you are just beginning your culinary journey or don't feel particularly inventive in the moment, the majority of these recipes are simple, quick to make and always healthful for your mind and body alike without compromising on unique, satisfying flavors. I recommend seasoning and sweetening the recipes as you desire, because everyone's palate is different.

Sauces, spices, salt and natural sweeteners help big time with flavor. Please adjust these recipes according to your own taste preferences. If a cookie recipe isn't sweet enough, add maple syrup or coconut sugar! If a savory dish doesn't have enough flavor for you, add a splash of lemon juice, a fat spoonful of creamy tahini and extra salt and pepper! You deserve to enjoy every bite of whatever you are eating.

RAW AND COOKED

I am a big fan of raw food, but I love cooked dishes just as much. For this reason, my diet is made up of both kinds of cuisine, and you'll find a variety of raw and cooked recipes in this book. Raw foods are fresh, hydrating, juicy and make for creamy, dreamy desserts, epic salads and nourishing, light meals. Cooked foods are cozy, comforting, filling and grounding for me. Plus there's something about baked goods that has me hooked. Some foods are more nutritious in their raw state (like berries and bell peppers), and others do more favors for ya when they're gently cooked (like kale and tomatoes). I keep this in mind when developing recipes in order to give you the best results for your taste buds and the rest of your bod. All my recipes are always 100% vegan and free from gluten for folks with celiac disease (of course, if you're into gluten, feel free to swap out the gluten-free options).

SUBSTITUTIONS AND ADAPTATIONS

I tend to have my personal favorite ingredients (ex. vanilla powder > vanilla extract, maple syrup > agave syrup, pecans > cashews, etc.) but we're all different, so go with what you have on hand or what you prefer. I am all for substitutions and adaptations because they make food more approachable and accessible for more folks.

NUTS	Substitute with any other nut, or hemp or sesame seeds.
SEEDS	Substitute with any other seed or nut.
NONDAIRY MILKS	Substitute with any other nondairy milk, or water if it's a smoothie recipe and you want a lighter drink.
NUT/SEED BUTTERS (INCLUDING COCONUT BUTTER)	Substitute with any other nut/seed butter, or if you are blending the recipe, you can use whole nuts/seeds. For a tablespoon of nut/seed butter, you'll need a small handful (scant ¼ cup) of nuts/seeds. Depending on the recipe, this may yield a less creamy result.
VANILLA POWDER	Substitute with pure vanilla extract.
SWEETENERS (INCLUDING DATES, MAPLE SYRUP, BROWN RICE SYRUP, COCONUT SUGAR)	Substitute with any other sweetener. If you need/want to replace stevia, use a couple tablespoons of an alternative sweetener (or a couple dates) for ⅛ teaspoon of stevia. I would not recommend replacing other sweeteners with stevia, because it will substantially alter the consistency/texture/volume of the recipe.
OILS	Most oils can be substituted for each other, but make sure that the oil you are cooking with is okay to use at higher temperatures. Also keep in mind that coconut oil and cocoa butter are solid at room temperature, while most other oils remain liquid.
CACAO POWDER	Substitute with cocoa powder or carob powder. Note that carob powder does have a very different flavor, so taste before using to see if you like it. I enjoy using a mixture of cacao/cocoa and carob sometimes to get the best of both.
BEANS/LEGUMES	Substitute with any other bean/legume, except in cases where color is relevant—then only substitute with like colors.
GRAINS/PSEUDO GRAINS	Substitute with any other grain/pseudo grain.

DRINKS

I'm a big fan of liquid nutrition. It's the quickest way to get in a ton of really powerful ingredients in delicious colorful forms. From tea to hot chocolate to green smoothies, these recipes are easy and fun to make, and can be enjoyed on-the-go in a jar or comfortably at home in a favorite cup (I love handmade ceramic mugs). In my drinks, I use adaptogens for their mood-boosting properties, anti-inflammatory spices like cinnamon and turmeric, antioxidant-rich fruits like berries and bananas, iron-rich greens like spinach and sometimes sneak in veggies like zucchini and beets because they add fiber and have anti-cancer benefits. Blending up nourishing and beautiful beverages is a satisfying way for me to spend time because I know the tonic I'm creating will help me feel good—in the long and short term—and taste great. I love observing the different consistencies and color tones of drinks; from creamy, thick, tan lattes to juicy, bright, fruity elixirs. Call me a freak (I certainly do . . . often), but I'm fascinated with the details of these textures: they're like sexy art. There is something so alive about them, and their ingredients allow me to feel that energy too. In short: I am amazed by the power of plants. These recipes are best enjoyed fresh. Cheers, y'all, to liiife!

NUT-FREE   SOY-FREE   RAW   QUICK TO MAKE

MATCHA FOR THE MORNINGS

Here's an elegant recipe that's satisfying to make. The ceremony of preparing and drinking matcha tea (that is, a type of green tea in powder form) is attributed to Zen Buddhism and spans back centuries. Most days I prefer to keep the recipe simple and semi-traditional by using only water and matcha, but you can dress it up however much you desire. Add creamy coconut, almond or oat milk, maple syrup and a splash of vanilla or almond extract for a delicious treat. Matcha contains antioxidants (specifically catechins which can help fight cancer and heart disease) and antiviral chlorophyll (which cleanses the liver and may help in cancer prevention and healing wounds). It gives me energy, without the headache often associated with caffeine consumption.

SERVES 1

½ tsp matcha tea powder, ideally ceremonial grade

3–4 oz (85–113 ml) hot water, just below boiling

1–2 tsp (5–10 ml) Ginger Syrup (page 219), or maple syrup

¼ cup (60 ml) Coconut Milk (page 209), as desired

¼ tsp vanilla extract

Sift the tea powder into a small bowl, and then whisk the water into the tea for 30 seconds until foamy and smooth.

Pour it into a small bowl or mug, stir in the syrup, milk and vanilla and sip mindfully before you get on with the day.

SOY-FREE

RAW

**QUICK
TO MAKE**

EARTHY IMMUNITY TONIC

This recipe has a rich, earthy, roasted flavor. It is not very sweet, which allows the tastes of the ingredients to shine through. Incidentally, those ingredients are top quality adaptogens which help to balance your hormones, strengthen immunity and alleviate anxiety and stress. In other words: GIMME.

Note: If you want it more like hot chocolate (and more caffeinated), add 1 to 2 teaspoons (2 to 5 g) of cacao nibs or cacao powder.

SERVES 1 TO 2

1½ cups (360 ml) strong-brewed white tea

1 tbsp (11 g) hazelnut butter

1 tsp maca powder

1 tsp ashwagandha powder

½ tsp reishi mushroom powder

½ tsp chaga mushroom powder

2 tsp (8g) coconut sugar, as desired

⅛ tsp cinnamon powder (optional)

⅛ tsp ginger powder (optional)

Pinch of stevia powder

Blend all the ingredients together until lusciously smooth. Adjust according to taste, adding more coconut sugar or stevia if you like.

Pour into a mug and enjoy! Best served warm.

NUT-FREE   SOY-FREE   RAW   QUICK TO MAKE

BERRY, BEET + GINGER SMOOTHIE WITH LIME

Beets offer a beautiful color to smoothies and, as long as you don't add too much, the flavor is wonderfully earthy. I like buying a big bag of beets from the farmers' market, using some in juice, some in my cooking and the rest for smoothies. I wash, scrub and chop them into 1-inch (2.5-cm) chunks and keep 'em in the freezer in a zip-top bag. Then it's effortless to throw in a small handful whenever I want a pink smoothie that has that extra nutritional boost. The lime juice and coconut water in this recipe cut through the sweetness of the fruit to make the drink a little lighter and refreshing.

SERVES 1 TO 2

SMOOTHIE

1 banana

1 cup (150 g) frozen strawberries

Scant ¼ cup (34 g) frozen, chopped red beet

1 tbsp (7 g) açaí berry powder

1 tsp ginger powder

1 cup (240 ml) coconut water (or nondairy milk or water)

1–2 tbsp (15–30 ml) lime juice

TOPPING

Mint leaves (optional)

Blend all the smoothie ingredients together until smooth, pink and delicious. Add the lime juice according to your taste preferences. I like things tangy.

Pour it into glasses, decorate with mint leaves if you like and enjoy!

NUT-FREE   SOY-FREE   RAW   QUICK
TO MAKE

TURMERIC + BLACK PEPPER ELIXIR

Turmeric has been used in Ayurvedic practices, Indian ceremony and Traditional Chinese Medicine (TCM) for thousands of years. Turmeric lattes have become a trend in Western cafes, but the drink owes homage to *haldi doodh*, a popular, warm turmeric milk recipe in India, used to soothe colds and other congestive ailments. I love making this in the evenings as I wind down from my day. The pepperine in black pepper increases the bioavailability of the curcumin in turmeric by 200 to 2000%, so I like to pair them together.

SERVES 1

1¼ cups (300 ml) hot water

1 tbsp (14 g) Coconut Butter (page 212)

½–¾ tsp turmeric powder, as desired

Pinch of ground black pepper

1 tsp coconut oil

¼ tsp ginger powder

Pinch of stevia powder

1 tsp maple syrup (optional)

Blend all the ingredients together until smooth. Adjust according to taste, adding more sweetener or spices if you desire.

Strain it through a nut milk bag, fine sieve or cheesecloth if you want it super smooth (but it's OK to drink without straining).

I love this warm, but it's delicious chilled as well.

SOY-FREE

RAW

**QUICK
TO MAKE**

JUICY GREEN PINEAPPLE SMOOTHIE
WITH MINT, BASIL + SPIRULINA

This is a light, hydrating and refreshing smoothie that's great on a hot day. I love citrus and the tanginess it lends to recipes, so please note that this is a pretty limey drink. If you aren't too keen on that, leave half of the lime out. I reckon some fresh ginger would be lovely added here, in case you have some around. Mint is excellent for helping with digestion (it tames an upset or bloated tummy). Spirulina is a blue-green algae and provides protein, iron, iodine, B12, beta-carotene, vitamin A and other good stuff. It's kinda magic, although the flavor may take some getting used to for some folks.

SERVES 1 TO 2

Blend all the smoothie ingredients together until smooth!

Throw some ice and mint leaves in a glass or two, pour in your smoothie and enjoy!

SMOOTHIE

⅔ cup (89 g) chopped cucumber

⅓ cup (13 g) packed mint leaves

⅓ cup (13 g) packed basil leaves

1 heaping cup (245 g) frozen pineapple chunks

½–1 tsp spirulina powder, as desired

1 lime, peeled and chopped

1 tsp maple syrup

½ cup (120 ml) water

½ cup (120 ml) nondairy milk (page 209)

ADDITIONS

2–4 ice cubes

1–2 tbsp (3–5 g) mint leaves

SOY-FREE

RAW

**QUICK
TO MAKE**

ALMOND ELDERFLOWER EMBRACE WITH CINNAMON

This recipe is inspired by a drink I had at a Lebanese restaurant downtown called Nuba; it was made with rose water and tasted divine. Here I use elderflower syrup so it still achieves that light, sweet, floral element. This is lovely served warm in the fall and winter, or chilled on ice during the hotter months.

SERVES 2

DRINK
2 cups (480 ml) nondairy milk
(page 209)

2 tbsp (30 ml) Elderflower Syrup
(page 220)

½ tsp cinnamon powder

Pinch of nutmeg powder

TOPPING
¼ tsp cinnamon powder

Blend all the drink ingredients together until smooth and delicious.

Pour into a glass or two, sprinkle on extra cinnamon and enjoy!

NUT-FREE   SOY-FREE   RAW   QUICK TO MAKE

LEMON GINGER FENNEL SLUSHIE WITH MANGO + BANANA

This drink is designed for folks of all genders during their period. Fennel and ginger have been proven to be highly effective in alleviating PMS symptoms (such as heavy flow, cramps and soreness), and I can personally attest to this. Peppermint tea also helps with bloating. Even if you aren't menstruating, this is a delicious, thick, frosty beverage anyone can appreciate.

SERVES 1 TO 2

¼ tsp fennel seeds

½–¾ tsp ginger powder, as desired

Scant ¾ cup (180 ml) Turmeric + Black Pepper Elixir (page 23)

1 tbsp (15 ml) lemon juice

1 cup (225 g) frozen banana

¾ cup (125 g) frozen mango

½ cup (120 ml) Coconut Milk (page 209)

1 tbsp (15 ml) maple syrup

Blend all the ingredients together until smooth and like a slushie. If it's too thick, add ¼ cup (60 ml) more of coconut milk. If it's too liquidy, add ¼ cup (41 g) more of frozen fruit. Adjust according to taste, adding more ginger, fennel or syrup if you like.

Pour it into a glass or two and enjoy!

NUT-FREE   SOY-FREE   RAW   QUICK
TO MAKE

SWEET REFRESH: PINEAPPLE BASIL JUICE

This, to me, is a bit of heaven on earth. It is the most refreshing, hydrating, naturally sweet and delicious drink I can imagine. Best served with lots of ice and slurped up in sunshine. Adding mint leaves would be a smart move here, and perhaps a lime.

SERVES 2

1 pineapple

⅓ cup (13 g) tightly packed basil leaves

1 cup (140 g) ice cubes

⅓ cup (80 ml) water (optional)

Put the pineapple and basil through your juicer, or blend it until smooth and strain through a sieve.

Pour it into glasses with ice, and if it's too sweet, just add some water to dilute the juice. Enjoy!

NUT-FREE **SOY-FREE** **RAW** **QUICK TO MAKE**

PINK LEMONADE

So, this has beet juice in it. If you're not a fan of beets, I know that info will be an immediate turnoff . . . but stay with me! The beet flavor is very subtle and actually works wonderfully snuck in alongside the citrusy sourness (lemons and lime) and sweetness (maple syrup and stevia). This is perfect served ice-cold in the summer. It's also lovely made with sparkling water or mild herbal tea-based kombucha.

SERVES 2 TO 4

DRINK

3 lemons

1 lime

¼ cup (39 g) chopped red beet

3–4 cups (710–940 ml) water; flat or sparkling

2 tbsp (30 ml) maple syrup

Scant 1 tsp stevia powder

ADD-ONS

1 cup (140 g) ice cubes

Peel and chop the citrus. Put the citrus and the beet through a juicer and strain through a fine sieve.

Add the water, and whisk or stir in the remaining ingredients. Adjust according to taste, adding more citrus, water or sweetener as desired.

Pour it into glasses and serve over ice!

SOY-FREE   RAW   QUICK
                   TO MAKE

BLUEBERRY, BRAZIL NUT + VANILLA SMOOTHIE

Blueberries are one of my top fave foods, no question. I am blessed enough to have five blueberry bushes in my fam's front yard, and every single summer I eagerly await their ripening. All season long, you can find me harvesting and eating 'em fresh, using them in recipes or storing in the freezer so I can enjoy their tart deliciousness all year. I think they pair perfectly with nuttiness and vanilla, so that's what we are doin' here. Brazil nuts are an excellent source of selenium, and blueberries provide antioxidants.

SERVES 1

1 cup (240 ml) water
1 cup (140 g) frozen blueberries
3 Brazil nuts
1 tbsp (11 g) almond butter
1 sliced apple or banana
½ tsp vanilla powder
Pinch of nutmeg
Pinch of stevia powder

Blend all the ingredients together until smooth. Adjust according to taste, adding a pinch more of nutmeg and/or stevia if desired.

Pour it into a cold glass and enjoy!

SOY-FREE

RAW

**QUICK
TO MAKE**

GOOD MOOD HOT CHOCOLATE

I say "Good Mood Hot Chocolate" because the ingredients—namely he shou wu, maca and ashwagandha—may help with regulating hormones, alleviating anxiety and encouraging relaxation. It's rich, satisfying and packs in a lot of traditional medicines for one comfy drink. I used to looove guzzling cups and cups of hot chocolate when I was younger, usually while camping 'cause that's just what ya do. Since discovering the world of powerful plant foods years ago, I now realize I can recreate those delicious, steamy mugs without experiencing a sugar crash later. This dairy-free recipe lifts my mood, promotes longevity and provides adaptogenic nourishment.

SERVES 1 TO 2

1½ cups (360 ml) hot water

1 tbsp (11 g) almond butter

Scant ¼ cup (43 g) pitted dates

1 heaping tbsp (7 g) cacao powder

1 heaping tsp maca powder

½ tsp ashwagandha powder

½ tsp he shou wu powder

⅛ tsp vanilla powder

¼ tsp cinnamon powder
(optional)

Pinch of sea salt

Blend all the ingredients until smooth. That's it! Best enjoyed fresh and hot. If you'd like a lighter version, simply blend in more water.

SOY-FREE   RAW

PUMPKIN PATCH SMOOTHIE

This is baaasically pumpkin pie in a glass, (*cue singing angels*), and it's inspired by a drink of the same name I enjoyed at a lovely li'l vegan cafe in north Vancouver called Buddha-Full. Pumpkin provides a whack-load of vitamin A, and the spices are anti-inflammatory. This is excellent when served with whipped coconut cream, Chewy Ginger Cookies (page 180) and a drizzle of molasses.

Note: You can switch out the pumpkin for sweet potato and the result is equally delicious; 10/10 would recommend.

SERVES 1 TO 2

SMOOTHIE
⅔ cup (160 ml) Coconut Milk (page 209)

⅔ cup (120 g) pumpkin purée

¼ cup (43 g) pitted dates

½ tsp cinnamon powder

¾ tsp fresh ginger

⅛–¼ tsp nutmeg powder

Pinch of stevia powder

Pinch of ground cloves

½ tsp vanilla extract

1 tsp melted coconut oil

1 tsp apple cider vinegar

4 medium ice cubes

GARNISH
1 tbsp (15 ml) blackstrap molasses

4 Chewy Ginger Cookies (page 180)

¼ cup (60 ml) Whipped Coconut Cream (page 206)

Pinch of cinnamon

To make the smoothie, blend all the ingredients together until smooth. Adjust according to taste, adding more sweetener, spices, etc. If you'd like it lighter, add more milk.

Serve in glasses decorated with your garnishes.

SOY-FREE   RAW   QUICK TO MAKE

ENERGIZING DAILY TONIC

I drink this thing almost every day and it has changed my world. The addition of medicinal mushrooms and other adaptogens to my diet has allowed my mood, energy and motivation to soar. This is a truly powerful tonic to manage my overall mental health (which benefits every other facet of my life). Plus, it tastes like a rich cuppa chocolaty coffee.

SERVES 1 TO 2

BASE
2–4 tbsp (14–28 g) vegan protein powder*

1 tbsp (7 g) maca powder

1 tsp ashwagandha powder

1 tsp mushroom blend powder**

1 tsp astragalus powder

¼ cup (30 g) pecans

2 Brazil nuts

2 cups (480 ml) hot water (or nondairy milk if you want it really creamy)

Pinch of stevia powder

1–2 tbsp (15–30 ml) maple syrup or dates (optional)

ADD-ONS
1 tbsp (7 g) cacao powder

1 tbsp (6 g) ground coffee

½ tsp vanilla extract

TOPPING
½ tsp apple pie spice mix, as desired***

Blend all the base ingredients except the maple syrup until smooth, creamy and delicious. Add 1 to 2 tablespoons (15 to 30 ml) of maple syrup or a small handful of dates, if you want it sweeter.

If you are using a plain protein powder, I'd recommend blending in the add-ons. The protein powder I use already has coffee and chocolate in it, so it provides a lot of delicious flavor. Don't use a gross-tasting protein powder! Vega's chocolate flavor is another good option, as is Nuzest.

Sprinkle with apple pie spice, if using, and enjoy!

*I love Nuzest's Clean Lean Protein in the chocolate or coffee flavor for this recipe.

**I use Harmonic Arts' 14 Mushroom Powder Steam Extract.

***Mine contains cinnamon, ginger, cardamom, nutmeg, cloves and orange peel.

NUT-FREE

SOY-FREE

RAW

PURE GREEN JUICE

I get "the glow" when I drink this juice regularly. It delivers a whackload of hydrating nutrition in an easily consumable form. If you wanna make juicing a habit, I would suggest making this recipe (or your fave juice recipe) in bigger batches and having it ready to go in your fridge over the next 3 days, or up to a week. It does lose its nutritional potency as time passes, but it's still going to add a boost to your day—and will be categorically better than the bottled stuff in the grocery store. If you need a sweeter juice, check out page 55, or add an apple to this recipe.

SERVES 1 TO 2; MAKES ~3 CUPS (710 ML)

1 lemon

1 tsp fresh ginger

1 cucumber

1 head lettuce

5 celery stalks

1 yellow bell pepper

Ice, as desired

Wash, peel and chop your produce.

Put all the ingredients, except the ice, through a juicer or blender.

If you are using a blender, strain the drink through a fine sieve (I'd recommend doing this even if you use a juicer, if you want super smooth juice).

Serve with ice and enjoy!

NUT-FREE

SOY-FREE

RAW

QUICK
TO MAKE

PROTEIN-PACKED VANILLA BANANA SHAKE

This drink is creamy, cold, sweet and somehow reminds me of banana bread. Hemp seeds are full of omega-3 and omega-6 fatty acids, and a decent amount of protein and iron. I love their nutty flavor, though for some it is a taste to be acquired. The tocotrienols I use are derived from stabilized rice bran and are rich in antioxidants, vitamins E, B and C. This is a great drink after a workout or to accompany breakfast. Feel free to add a handful of berries or greens for an extra boost.

SERVES 1 TO 2; MAKES ~3 CUPS (710 ML)

2 cups (480 ml) Rice Milk (page 210)

2 tbsp (14 g) hemp protein powder, or 3 tbsp (30 g) hemp seeds

2 tbsp (14 g) tocotrienols

2 pitted dates

Pinch of sea salt

½ tsp vanilla powder

Pinch of stevia powder

1 frozen banana

1 tbsp (11 g) Coconut Butter (page 212)

2–4 ice cubes, as desired

Blend all the ingredients, except the ice, until smooth. Add ice if you want it colder and lighter. If you'd like it a bit sweeter, add another date. If you want more vanilla, add more vanilla!

Pour it into glasses and enjoy!

SOY-FREE   RAW   QUICK TO MAKE

PMS POTION

This is basically sweet potato pie in a cold, creamy shake. This recipe includes ginger and fennel, which help to alleviate cramps and blood loss during one's menstrual cycle. It also contains iron (in the tahini) and vitamin C (in the lemon juice). People lose iron during their periods, so it's important to replenish that. Vitamin C helps with iron absorption.

SERVES 1 TO 2; MAKES ~3 CUPS (710 ML)

1½ cups (360 ml) nondairy milk (page 209)

⅓ cup (60 g) sweet potato purée

1 frozen banana

2 tbsp (30 g) tahini

1 tsp lemon juice

½ tsp cinnamon powder

2 cloves

⅛ tsp turmeric powder

¼ tsp fennel seeds

¼ tsp ginger powder

Pinch of stevia powder

Maple syrup, as desired

4–5 ice cubes, as desired

Blend all the ingredients until smooth. Adjust it according to taste, adding maple syrup, extra spices and ice, as desired.

Pour it into a cup and enjoy!

SOY-FREE   QUICK
TO MAKE

ROASTED CHICORY LATTE

Chicory root has a wonderful roasty, rich flavor that reminds some people of coffee. I'm not a coffee drinker, but I love what chicory adds to creamy lattes. Chicory is a prebiotic food, which means it feeds the beneficial bacteria living in your gut. If chicory is not your fave, I would recommend trying a coffee alternative called Dandy Blend. It includes chicory, but not as the main ingredient. The blend is delicious in its own right, and all my friends who regularly drink coffee didn't even realize it was coffee- and caffeine-free when I made a pot for them to try.

SERVES 1

1 tbsp (6 g) roasted chicory root, or Dandy Blend

1 cup (240 ml) boiling water

2–4 pitted dates, as desired

1 tbsp (11 g) almond butter

Pinch of stevia, if needed

½ tsp cinnamon powder

½ tsp mucuna pruriens powder

½ cup (120 ml) nondairy milk (page 209), or more as desired

Blend all the ingredients until smooth, about a minute. If you'd like it richer and creamier, add more almond butter. If you'd like it lighter, add more milk. Best served fresh with all that foam!

NUT-FREE **SOY-FREE** **RAW** **QUICK TO MAKE**

CREAMY GREEN SMOOTHIE

Chia seeds add fiber and nutrition here, but most importantly make the whole drink creamy and thick. The green powders (plus spinach) pack in a ton of good stuff for your body and brain; including iron, antioxidants, vitamins A, K and C and chlorophyll.

SERVES 1 TO 2

1½ cups (360 ml) Rice Milk (page 210)

1 frozen banana

1 tsp moringa powder

1 tsp spirulina powder

1 tsp matcha powder

2 cups (80 g) spinach leaves, or as desired

2 tsp (7 g) chia seeds

2 tsp (10 ml) lemon juice

Pinch of stevia powder

2 pitted dates

Ice cubes, as desired

Blend all the ingredients until smooth, adding ice as needed to get the consistency you want. Adjust according to taste, adding extra sweetener if you like. Some vanilla might also be nice here.

Pour it into a glass and enjoy!

NUT-FREE   SOY-FREE   RAW   QUICK TO MAKE

PANDAN CARDAMOM LATTE

Pandan tea leaves have a special scent and taste that remind me of vanilla wafers. In fact, pandan is often used to flavor cakes and rice, or served with dessert, in Southeast Asian countries like Thailand and Vietnam. I was fortunate enough to be introduced to lemongrass pandan tea at a vegan Vietnamese restaurant called Veggie Bowl where they sold bags of it. Simply smelling the jar of dry tea in my tea drawer is a wonderfully sensual experience. I find that pandan's flavor profile works perfectly with aromatic cardamom, and is enhanced by a li'l extra vanilla. This is a fantastically foamy drink.

SERVES 1

1 cup (240 ml) strong-brewed lemongrass pandan tea (hot or cold)

½ cup (120 ml) Rice Milk (page 210)

¼ tsp vanilla powder

2–4 pitted dates

Pinch of ground cardamom, as desired

Pinch of ginger powder, as desired

Pinch of ground nutmeg, as desired

½ tsp coconut oil

Pinch of sea salt

Pinch of stevia powder, as desired

Blend all the ingredients together until smooth and foamy. Adjust according to taste, adding extra spices and/or sweetener.

Pour it into a mug and enjoy! Sprinkle with extra nutmeg if desired.

NUT-FREE   SOY-FREE   RAW

SWEET GREEN JUICE

This recipe is for when you want that fresh, green flavor (Is it the taste of chlorophyll, or what? Genuinely curious . . .) plus some fruity goodness. Use any other greens instead of bok choy, if you want.

SERVES 1 TO 2

1 cucumber
1 lb (455 g) bok choy
1 lemon
1 apple
1 tbsp (14 g) fresh ginger
1 yellow bell pepper
1 orange
Ice, as desired

Wash, peel and chop your produce.

Put all the ingredients, except the ice, through a juicer or blender.

If you are using a blender, strain the drink through a fine sieve (I'd recommend doing this even if you use a juicer, if you want super smooth juice).

Serve with ice and enjoy!

DANDELION CHOCOLATE ICED LATTE WITH GINGER SYRUP

This tastes like iced chocolate milk. The ginger adds a spicy component after the earthy flavor of the cacao passes. Like chicory, dandelion tea is sometimes used as a coffee replacement because it provides a robust, roasted flavor. It's also really helpful with easing digestion and increasing bile flow, which is good for your liver. It is a prebiotic (also like chicory), so it helps keep your gut happy. Dandelion has a diuretic effect and provides potassium. If you want to try a delicious dandelion tea drink mix that also contains chicory, as well as rye and barley, I'd highly recommend Dandy Blend.

SERVES 1

1 cup (240 ml) chilled, strong-brewed dandelion tea (strained or unstrained)

½ cup (120 ml) Oat Milk (page 210)

½ tsp coconut oil

¼ tsp vanilla powder

1 tsp cacao powder

½ tsp chaga mushroom powder

1 tbsp (25 g) Ginger Syrup (page 219), or 1–2 pitted dates

¼–½ tsp ginger powder, as desired

Pinch of stevia powder

Ice cubes, as desired

Blend together all the ingredients, except the ice, adding ginger according to your preference. If you'd like it sweeter, use more ginger syrup or throw in a couple of pitted dates.

Pour it into a glass filled with ice cubes. Enjoy!

NUT-FREE   SOY-FREE   RAW

SAVORY TOMATO VEGGIE JUICE

Here's the easiest way to get in all your veggies—and more!—for the day. In fact, a lot of these "veggies" are non-sweet fruits (like cucumber, tomato and bell pepper). This drink is packed with antioxidants, vitamins C and A, along with decent amounts of calcium and iron. Think V8, but homemade and less processed. This recipe was inspired by one from the ever-informative author and podcaster Michael Greger, MD FACLM and founder of Nutritionfacts.org. His website, podcast and books provide thoroughly researched advice on how to eat the most powerful foods available to maximize physical well-being and fight preventable disease.

SERVES 2 TO 3

3 plum tomatoes

2 carrots

3 celery stalks

½ cucumber

1 lemon

1 tbsp (14 g) chunk ginger

1 red bell pepper

3 cups (120 g) kale

1 garlic clove (optional)

1 apple (optional)

Ice cubes (optional)

Wash, peel and chop the produce as needed.

Put everything through a juicer, alternating between more fibrous and juicier foods to keep the juicer running smoothly. If you don't mind garlic, add the garlic. If you'd like it sweeter, add an apple and other sweet fruits if needed.

Strain if desired, then serve with ice or at room temperature.

This is best enjoyed fresh, but this will keep for up to 3 days in the fridge.

SPICY SHOT WITH LEMON, TURMERIC, PEPPER + GINGER

Drink this when you need a shot of some immune-boosting ingredients or a spicy, tart pick-me-up. Feel free to adapt the amounts according to your own taste preferences.

SERVES 4 TO 5

¼ cup (60 ml) lemon juice

1 tbsp (14 g) chunk turmeric

1 tbsp (14 g) chunk ginger

½ tsp cayenne powder

¼ tsp cracked black pepper

1 cup (240 ml) water (hot or cold), as needed

1–2 tbsp (15–30 ml) maple syrup, as needed

Blend all the ingredients together until smooth, and then strain it through a cheesecloth, a fine sieve or a nut milk bag. Note: it may stain because of the turmeric. Adjust the water and sweetener as needed to make it palatable. Alternatively, make this in a big batch and put the lemon, turmeric and ginger through your juicer; then blend it with the other ingredients.

Pour it into shot glasses and enjoy. This will keep for a week in the fridge.

NUT-FREE **SOY-FREE** **RAW** **QUICK TO MAKE**

FRUIT PUNCH

The "punch" in this drink comes from apple cider vinegar; it's an acquired taste but actually quite lovely when balanced among fruity sweetness and ice, as it is here. Apple cider vinegar has a lot of benefits for your gut health, since it's a fermented food and rich in enzymes. I add a splash to my water every morning. This recipe is inspired by one that a friend—also named Emily—had me try years ago. If you don't like coconut water, use sparkling or flat water.

SERVES 1 TO 2

3 cups (710 ml) coconut water (or water)

1 tbsp (15 ml) apple cider vinegar, or more as desired

¼ cup (60 ml) cranberry juice

¼ cup (60 ml) pomegranate juice

¼ cup (60 ml) beet juice

2 tbsp (30 ml) maple syrup, as desired

Pinch of stevia powder (optional)

Ice cubes, as desired

Smashed berries (optional)

Basil (optional)

Vigorously stir or whisk together all the ingredients except the ice until evenly combined, adding apple cider vinegar and maple syrup to taste. If you want a sweet aftertaste, add a pinch of stevia.

Serve with plenty of ice, and perhaps some smashed berries and basil leaves. Best fresh.

SOY-FREE RAW QUICK TO MAKE

QUICK ADAPTOGENIC CHOCOLATE MILK

This is delicious hot or cold. I make the chocolate mix in big batches to have ready to go in my cupboard whenever I want chocolate milk or hot chocolate with mood-boosting, anti-anxiety qualities.

SERVES 1

2 tbsp (14 g) Adaptogenic Chocolate Mix (page 257)

½ tsp coconut oil

1 cup (240 ml) nondairy milk (page 209)

2 pitted dates, as desired

Blend all the ingredients until smooth. Add dates if you'd like it sweeter! Add more almond milk if you like.

This is best enjoyed right away, but will keep in the fridge for 1 to 2 days. Just give it a good shake before drinking if you've let it sit for awhile.

NUT-FREE   SOY-FREE   RAW   QUICK
                                     TO MAKE

QUICK TURMERIC MILK

I try to consume turmeric every day because of its incredible health benefits. Pairing it with black pepper, as I do in my turmeric spice mix, ups its absorption rate by 200 to 2000%. This is the quickest way to get it in my bod on those days I don't feel like getting out a bunch of jars and spices.

SERVES 1

1–2 tbsp (7–14 g) Turmeric Spice Mix (page 258), as desired

½ tsp (120 ml) coconut oil

1 cup (240 ml) Coconut Milk (page 209)

2 pitted dates, as desired

Blend all the ingredients until smooth, adding the turmeric mix to taste. Add dates if you'd like it sweeter. Add more coconut milk if you like.

This is best enjoyed right away, but will keep in the fridge for 1 to 2 days. Just give it a good shake before drinking if you've let it sit for awhile.

NUT-FREE   SOY-FREE   RAW   QUICK TO MAKE

QUICK GREEN POWER SHAKE

Edible, green, leafy things are some of the healthiest foods we can eat: they are positively packed with nutrition and fiber. I value them in concentrated powder form and in their whole state. This recipe is a super easy way to get in a varied dose of a number of different greens with just a handful of ingredients.

SERVES 1

1–2 tbsp (7–14 g) Green Power Mix (page 261), as desired

1 cup (240 ml) Hemp Milk (page 209)

1 cup (140 g) ice cubes, or more as desired

1 cup (250 g) pineapple

1 cup (40 g) dark, leafy greens*

2 pitted dates, as desired

*Spinach, kale, bok choy, yu choy, carrot greens, beet greens or swiss chard

Blend all the ingredients until smooth, adding the greens mix to taste. Add dates if you'd like it sweeter. Add more hemp milk if you like.

This one's best enjoyed right away.

SAVORY MAINS

Ah, the big event. These filling meals will satisfy and nourish at the same time. I have made sure to include a decent amount of protein in these recipes, along with a variety of colorful veggies and healthy fats . . . so rest assured you're getting everything your body needs. We are eating the rainbow in this chapter, and that means lots of antioxidant-rich foods and phytochemicals, which can help to protect against cancer. Inevitably, these same ingredients tend to be high in fiber and offer iron, vitamin C, A, B and K, magnesium, zinc and more. I love flavorful sauces, garlic, sesame oil, roasted sweet potatoes, fresh basil and cilantro, lemon juice and vinegars, creamy and crunchy textures combined, smoked salt, tahini and spinach. Get ready for a lot of those. These meals vary from simple everyday basics, to more impressive recipes for when you want to spend some more time in the kitchen (maybe with a glass of red wine nearby and your fave album playing?). Whatever the plan is, I'm in. Let's go.

ZUCCHINI NOODLES WITH PUMPKIN SEED PESTO, ROASTED TOMATOES + TAHINI CHICKPEA CAKES

Pesto is an important part of my life, and you absolutely do not need Parmesan cheese to make it taste amazing. A good pesto is full of fresh basil, garlic, olive oil and nuttiness from pine nuts or whatever other fatty nut or seed you like. In this case, I have used a mix of Brazil nuts (very high in selenium), pistachios and pumpkin seeds. Zucchini noodles are a popular component to many raw dishes, but feel free to use whatever pasta you want. Zucchini noodles just make for a lighter, more hydrating meal. I've learned that to prepare them for recipes I need to let them sit and dry out a little bit, so when I add a sauce later, it doesn't become a soggy, wet mess. Zucchinis are a whole, fresh veggie and thus they are carrying a LOT of water, so it makes a huge difference when you let some of it drain off before throwing the noodles in a recipe.

SERVES 1 TO 2, + LEFTOVER PESTO

ROASTED TOMATOES

3 roma tomatoes

1 tbsp (15 ml) extra-virgin olive oil (optional)

ZUCCHINI NOODLES

2 small to medium zucchinis

PESTO

½ cup (76 g) Brazil nuts

½ cup (62 g) pistachios

½ cup (32 g) pumpkin seeds

1 cup (40 g) packed basil leaves

1 cup (40 g) packed cilantro leaves

¾ cup (180 ml) extra-virgin olive oil

3 garlic cloves

¼ cup (60 ml) lemon juice

1 tsp sea salt

1 tsp cracked black pepper

To roast the tomatoes, preheat the oven to 400°F (204°C). Slice the tomatoes into quarters and drizzle in a little olive oil, if using. Roast for 15 to 20 minutes, or until their juices are bubbling out and their skin is wrinkly. They should smell divine.

To make the noodles, shred the zucchini into strips using a cheese grater, spiral slicer or mandoline. Put all the noodles into a colander and place the colander in a larger bowl; set aside while you make the rest of the recipe. This will allow the excess moisture in the zucchinis to drain so that when you coat them in pesto, it doesn't become a soup.

To make the pesto, throw all the ingredients in a food processor and process until evenly ground into a thick pesto. Adjust according to your taste preferences, adding more salt or garlic if you like. Note: we want to leave the pesto a bit thick because the zucchini noodles will lend a lot of moisture to the recipe. So if you are tempted to add extra olive oil or more lemon juice here, hold off for now.

(continued)

ZUCCHINI NOODLES WITH PUMPKIN SEED PESTO, ROASTED TOMATOES + TAHINI CHICKPEA CAKES (CONTINUED)

CHICKPEA CAKES
2 cups (330 g) cooked chickpeas

3 tbsp (45 ml) lemon juice

¼ cup (60 g) tahini

½ tsp sea salt

½ tsp cracked black pepper

1 tbsp (15 ml) extra-virgin olive oil, + more for cooking

¼ tsp chipotle powder

1 tsp cumin powder

TOPPINGS
2 tsp (3 g) pumpkin seeds

½ tsp cracked black pepper

To make the chickpea cakes, mash the chickpeas into a thick, clumpy paste by hand with a fork or potato masher, or in a food processor. Stir in the rest of the ingredients until you have a thick, savory dough-like mixture. Scoop it into cakes with an ice-cream scoop or by hand. I like my cakes to be about the size of my palm, and around an inch (2.5-cm) thick. Drizzle a teaspoon of olive oil into a nonstick pan on low or medium-low heat, and let it warm up for a minute. To "fry" your cakes, cook them in the pan for 3 to 5 minutes on each side. They should get brown and crispy. Add more oil as needed.

Coat the noodles in as much pesto as you desire. Scoop the noodles onto plates or in bowls, add the chickpea cakes and tomatoes and sprinkle everything with some more pumpkin seeds and cracked black pepper.

SOY-FREE

ZUCCHINI GARLIC CAKES WITH CORN SALSA + SMOKY TOMATO SAUCE + PUMPKIN SEEDS

Zucchini has become one of my favorite foods. Since its flavor, texture and color are not particularly intense, I can turn it into so many different things. Here we use them as a base for savory cakes, which pair wonderfully with a tangy salad and sauce. Spinach is a great source of iron, vitamin K and carotenoids (vitamin A), which are necessary for blood health; and all the spices in this recipe have anti-inflammatory and anti-cancer properties.

SERVES 3 TO 4

ZUCCHINI GARLIC CAKES
2 cups (225 g) grated zucchini

1 cup (120 g) walnuts

2 cups (80 g) spinach

2 tbsp (30 ml) lime juice

1 tbsp (7 g) garlic powder

1 tsp sea salt

1 tsp cracked black pepper

1 tsp ground coriander

½ tsp cumin powder

Heaping ¾ cup (100 g) chickpea flour

Heaping ½ cup (40 g) nutritional yeast

1–2 tbsp (15–30 ml) extra-virgin olive oil, for cooking

To make the cakes, put all the ingredients in a food processor—except the chickpea flour, nutritional yeast and olive oil—and process until you have a chunky mush. Add the chickpea flour and nutritional yeast, and then process once more so everything is evenly blended.

Heat up a bit of olive oil in a large nonstick pan on medium or medium-low heat. It should be hot enough that when you place in a cake, it immediately begins to sizzle.

Form your batter into balls or cakes (I use an ice cream scoop and then pat them down into patties) and cook on medium-low heat, about 5 minutes for each side. They should hold together and become a dark, crispy brown once done.

(continued)

ZUCCHINI GARLIC CAKES WITH CORN SALSA + SMOKY TOMATO SAUCE + PUMPKIN SEEDS (CONTINUED)

SMOKY TOMATO SAUCE
1 cup (240 ml) tomato purée

¼ tsp chipotle powder

¼ tsp smoked paprika

¼ tsp cayenne powder

½–¾ tsp cumin powder, as desired

1 tbsp (15 ml) blackstrap molasses

1 tbsp (15 ml) tamari

1 tsp garlic powder

1 tsp apple cider vinegar

CHEESE
1 cup (110 g) cashews

½ cup (75 g) Brazil nuts

1 tbsp (15 ml) lemon juice

2 tsp (5 g) herbes de provence

1 tsp garlic powder

2 tbsp (34 g) miso paste

Water, as needed

CORN SALSA
2 cups (290 g) sweet corn kernels

2 cups (320 g) chopped heirloom tomatoes

⅓ cup (13 g) chopped cilantro

⅓ cup (13 g) chopped basil

1 tbsp (15 ml) extra-virgin olive oil

2 tbsp (30 ml) lime juice

Salt and pepper, to taste

ADD-ONS
Lime wedges

Chopped herbs, like cilantro and basil

To make the smoky tomato sauce, blend all the ingredients until smooth.

To make the cheese, blend all the ingredients until smooth. It's ready right away, or let it sit out for 24 hours to develop some sharper notes.

To make the salsa, throw everything together and add salt and pepper to taste.

To assemble, scoop the salsa onto plates, top with your cakes and serve with your sauce and cheese. This is excellent with lime wedges and extra chopped herbs; they take this dish to the next level.

BAKED SWEET POTATOES WITH YU CHOY, SHREDDED CARROT, RED PEPPER, TOFU + SPICES

This is a simple meal that's full of flavor and color. You can really use any veggies you like. Yu choy is one of my favorite greens: it happens to carry a fantastic amount of vitamins A and C, plus a bit of calcium.

SERVES 1 TO 2

VEG
2 sweet potatoes
2 cups (80 g) yu choy
1 red bell pepper
¾ cup (190 g) smoked tofu
1 carrot
1 clove garlic
1 tbsp (14 g) ginger root

SAUCE
½ tsp cumin powder
½ tsp Madras curry powder
½ tsp chipotle powder
½ tsp paprika powder
⅛ tsp cracked black pepper
1 tsp tamari
1 tsp maple syrup
2 tbsp (30 ml) extra-virgin olive oil
1 tbsp (15 ml) rice vinegar

TOPPINGS
¼ cup (45 g) tahini
⅓ cup (10 g) packed basil leaves
¼ cup (30 g) chopped walnuts
Salt and pepper, to taste

Preheat the oven to 375°F (190°C). Wash and scrub the sweet potatoes, then bake them (no need to cut them or add anything) for 30 to 40 minutes, or until they are soft all the way through and starting to bubble up juices.

Roughly chop the yu choy, pepper and tofu. Shred the carrot. Grate the garlic and ginger. Set aside.

Heat a pan on medium-low heat. Whisk together all the sauce ingredients and pour it into the pan. Add the veg and stir-fry until vibrantly colored and softened to your preference, about 10 to 15 minutes.

To assemble, place the sweet potatoes in two bowls or on two plates and make a deep cut in the center so you can fill the sweet potatoes with your veggies. Add your stir-fried veg and top with the tahini, basil and walnuts. If you'd like more salt or pepper, add as desired.

TOFU SCRAM WITH ROASTED ROSEMARY SWEET POTATOES, BROCCOLI + AVO TOAST

Some days I just crave a big bowl of savory goodness in the form of roasted veggies, some hearty plant-based protein and a lot of spice. This is a perfect example. Sweet potatoes are chock-full of vitamin A, which is vital for skin and eye health; broccoli is a wonder food, packed with vitamins K and C, insoluble fiber and iron; avocados provide healthy monounsaturated fats; and tofu is an excellent source of protein and calcium. The spices used in this recipe are terrific for their anti-cancer properties and ability to fight inflammation; and the walnut turmeric sauce paired with sweet potato is a match made in heaven.

SERVES 2 TO 3

SWEET POTATOES

2 large sweet potatoes, peeled and chopped into 1-inch (2.5-cm) cubes

1 tbsp (15 ml) rosemary-infused extra-virgin olive oil

½ tsp cracked black pepper

1 tbsp (15 ml) apple cider vinegar

1 tsp dried rosemary

TOFU SCRAM

1 tbsp (15 ml) extra-virgin olive oil

1 tbsp (15 ml) apple cider vinegar

1 tsp tamari

1 tsp maple syrup

1 tsp Madras curry powder

½ tsp turmeric powder

½ tsp coriander powder

½ tsp chipotle powder

½ tsp smoked paprika powder

½ tsp cracked black pepper

1 cup (250 g) firm tofu, crumbled into bite-size pieces

2 cups (310 g) small broccoli florets

TOPPINGS

Salt, to taste

½ batch Walnut Turmeric Sauce (page 238)

¼ cup (10 g) chopped basil leaves

2 tsp sunflower seeds

2 tsp pumpkin seeds

Avocado toast, to serve

To roast the sweet potatoes, first preheat the oven to 400°F (204°C). Toss the sweet potatoes with the olive oil, pepper, vinegar and rosemary until evenly coated. Bake on a parchment paper–lined pan for 25 minutes, and then flip all the pieces over. Bake for another 10 to 15 minutes, or until the pieces are starting to look brown and crisp on the edges. Take them out of the oven and set aside.

Now make the tofu scram. In a large sauté pan on medium heat, add the oil, vinegar, tamari, syrup, and dry spices and herbs. Add the crumbled tofu to the pan and gently cover it evenly in the spices and oil. Add the broccoli and do the same. Sauté for 8 to 10 minutes or until the broccoli is a vibrant green color and softened to your liking. Add the baked sweet potato pieces and stir everything up once more. Scoop it onto plates or into bowls, adding salt and sauce to taste, and top with chopped basil and sunflower and pumpkin seeds. Serve with avocado toast on the side.

SOY-FREE   QUICK
             TO MAKE

GARLICKY GREENS WITH BAKED SWEET POTATO, PECANS, SESAME OIL + QUINOA

Cooking greens in olive oil with spices, garlic and onion is a magnificent way to get more of them in your diet. Dark leafy greens are some of the most nutritious foods on earth, and consuming them regularly has huge benefits. They contain loads of vitamins A, K and C. Foods like spinach and kale can help prevent cancer along with lowering blood pressure and cholesterol. Another big plus is that when you cook them, they shrink down to almost nothing and their texture becomes buttery.

SERVES 2

GARLICKY GREENS

2 tbsp (30 ml) extra-virgin olive oil

½ tsp sea salt

½ tsp ground coriander

3 tsp (9 g) peeled and chopped garlic

½ cup (75 g) peeled and chopped white onion

5 oz (140 g) spinach leaves

5 oz (140 g) kale leaves

3 oz (85 g) swiss chard leaves

1 tsp apple cider vinegar

1 cup (170 g) cooked black bean flakes

1 cup (110 g) cooked quinoa

1 baked sweet potato, sliced in half lengthwise

¼ cup (30 g) chopped pecans

2 tsp (10 ml) sesame oil

2 tbsp (30 g) tahini

Salt and pepper, to taste

To make the greens, heat the oil, salt and coriander in a pan on medium-low heat. Add the garlic and onion and sauté until translucent and aromatic, about 2 or 3 minutes. Turn the heat down to low and add the greens and vinegar. Sauté until they are vibrant green and softened, about 3 to 5 minutes.

Assemble your bowls. Mix together the black bean flakes and quinoa, scoop it into bowls or onto plates, add half a sweet potato and then top with your greens.

Sprinkle on the chopped pecans and drizzle on the sesame oil and tahini. Add salt and pepper according to taste.

QUICK BROCCOLI SPINACH SOUP
WITH SESAME + AVOCADO

This recipe is a delicious, super quick and foolproof way to get in your cruciferous veggies for the day. Broccoli and its relatives—cabbage, kale, etc.—are *so good* for us, providing serious amounts of a number of nutrients, vitamins and fiber. There is much controversy over many foods, but basically everyone agrees that including more greens in our diet is a good idea. When I can't be bothered to cook for an hour because I am tired or too busy, but haven't had my kick of greens for the day, I make this soup.

SERVES 2 TO 3; MAKES ~4 CUPS (945 ML)

SOUP

2 cups (310 g) packed broccoli florets

2 cups (80 g) packed spinach

1 tsp garlic powder

½ tsp cumin powder

½ tsp ground coriander

½ tsp herbes de provence

¼ tsp ginger powder

Salt and pepper, as desired

1 tbsp (15 ml) lemon juice

1 tbsp (15 ml) extra-virgin olive oil (optional)

1 cup (240 ml) vegetable broth, or water

TOPPINGS

2 tbsp (30 g) tahini

2 tsp (10 ml) sesame oil

1 tbsp (10 g) sesame seeds

1 sliced avocado

ADD-ONS

1 cup (165 g) Spiced Chickpeas (page 232)

½ cup (125 g) sliced, steamed tofu

To make the soup, steam the broccoli and spinach for 7 minutes, or until vibrantly green and just slightly softened.

Add them and all the other soup ingredients to a blender; blend until smooth. Adjust according to taste, adding more spices if desired.

Pour it into bowls and decorate with the tahini, sesame oil, seeds and avocado.

If you would like a more filling and protein-rich bowl, add chickpeas or tofu.

QUICK
TO MAKE

CHICKPEA YU CHOY STIR-FRY WITH
BAKED KABOCHA + HERBED GRAVY

Yu choy, a Chinese green, is one my favorite foods. Its texture, color, shape and flavor are delicious. Yu choy is often sautéed with cooking oil, garlic and soy sauce, and then served with white pepper and sesame oil. In this recipe, I pair it with kabocha squash, which has an incredible melt-in-your-mouth texture and sweet, nutty flavor.

SERVES 3

SQUASH
1 small kabocha squash

1–2 tbsp (15–30 ml) extra-virgin olive oil, as desired

Salt and pepper, as desired

STIR-FRY
1 tbsp (14 g) coconut oil

½ tsp ground coriander

½ tsp cumin powder

¼ tsp cracked black pepper

2 cloves garlic, chopped

1 small onion, chopped

1 tbsp (15 ml) tamari

½ cup (82 g) cooked chickpeas

3 cups (90 g) yu choy, chopped

3 cups (90 g) spinach

1 green onion, chopped

1 tbsp (15 ml) lemon juice

TOPPINGS
½ batch Rosemary + Thyme Gravy (page 247)

½ cup (60 g) walnuts, chopped

Preheat the oven to 400°F (204°C).

To bake the squash, cut the squash into wedges (leave the seeds or take them out, up to you) and place on a parchment paper–lined baking sheet. Drizzle in the oil, and sprinkle with salt and pepper. Bake for 30 minutes, or until the wedges are just starting to brown. Then flip them and bake for another 10 minutes, or until they are brown and a fork easily goes through them.

To make the stir-fry, heat the oil and spices in a pan on medium-low heat. Add the garlic and onion and cook for about 5 minutes, or until they're very aromatic and beginning to brown. Lower the heat, add the tamari and chickpeas, and cook for another 2 minutes. Then add the yu choy, spinach, green onion and lemon juice. Cook for another 3 to 5 minutes or until the greens are tender and vibrantly colored.

Scoop the stir-fry into bowls or onto plates, add a few kabocha wedges on top, and drizzle everything in the gravy. Add walnut pieces for a crunch.

ROASTED CARROT + CAULIFLOWER SOUP

Warm, salted, roasted vegetables are such a comforting food to create, smell and savor. Here I've simply blended some of my favorites up into a creamy bowl of soup. Lovely in the winter with fresh sourdough bread, and chilly weather outside.

SERVES 4 TO 6

SOUP
2 small onions

2 garlic cloves

1 small head cauliflower

5 carrots

Extra-virgin olive oil, as desired

½ tsp ground coriander

½ tsp cracked black pepper

¼ tsp turmeric powder

1 cup (240 ml) Coconut Milk (page 209)

4 cups (940 ml) vegetable broth

Sea salt, as desired

TOPPINGS
Roasted vegetables

Sesame oil

Nuts or seeds

Spiced Chickpeas (page 232)

Preheat the oven to 400°F (204°C).

Peel and chop the onions and garlic. Roughly chop the cauliflower and slice the carrots lengthwise. Drizzle the vegetables in olive oil, and sprinkle with the coriander, pepper and turmeric.

Bake for 40 minutes, or until the veggies start to brown. Flip and bake for another 20 minutes or until tender and browning.

Blend the veggies with the coconut milk, vegetable broth and salt. If you want your soup chunky, reserve some cauliflower and carrots here.

Pour into bowls, add your veggies (if you saved some) or other roasted veg, drizzle on some sesame oil or other toppings like crunchy seeds or Spiced Chickpeas (page 232) and enjoy.

NUT-FREE **SOY-FREE** **QUICK TO MAKE**

BIG OLE SALAD WITH CHICKPEAS, SHREDDED VEG + CHEESY CRACKERS

Contrary to some popular, pessimistic beliefs about salad as a meal, I promise this recipe is substantial and filling on those days that find you craving fresh crunch and big flavor.

SERVES 2

1 head romaine lettuce

1 green onion

1 carrot

1 beet

3 cups (120 g) broccoli florets

Lemon Tahini Poppy Seed Dressing (page 241)

1 cup (110 g) cooked quinoa

1 cup (172 g) Spiced Chickpeas (page 232)

Paprika Garlic Crackers (page 228), as desired

To prep the salad, chop up the lettuce and green onion, and shred the carrot and beet. Set them aside.

Steam the broccoli and green onion for 5 minutes, or until slightly tender and vibrantly green.

Add the dressing to your lettuce, as desired, and mix in evenly.

Throw all the other goodies on top and enjoy!

SOY-FREE

QUICK TO MAKE

PASTA WITH WALNUT CILANTRO PESTO + AVOCADO

Sometimes I crave a large bowl of carbs, but also want the benefits of a bit of greens. This dish is perfect for these times. If you want a fresh, crunchy side, pair with salad. If you'd like more protein, serve with Chickpea Cakes (page 74).

SERVES 2 TO 3

PASTA
7–11 oz (200–300 g) gluten-free pasta
1 tbsp (15 ml) extra-virgin olive oil
Pinch of salt

TOPPINGS
Walnut Cilantro Pesto (page 248)
½ avocado

Cook the pasta to the tenderness you desire.

Toss the pasta with the olive oil and salt, and then coat in the pesto.

Serve with sliced avocado.

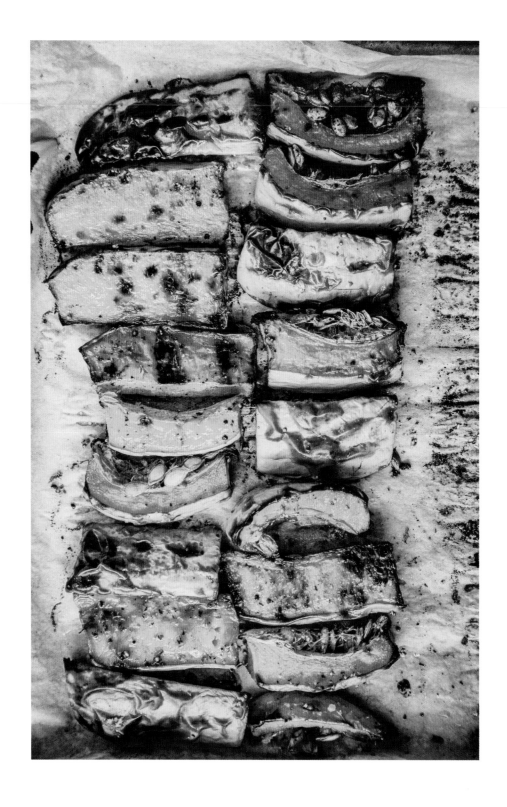

QUINOA SQUASH CAKES WITH MAPLE DIJON SAUCE, PECANS + ASPARAGUS

This is a rich, colorful, fully-flavored meal that I crave on fall and winter evenings. The Maple Dijon Dressing adds a tart, sweet layer to the savory cakes and vegetables. Naturally gluten-free, quinoa (it's a seed, not a grain!) is high in fiber, magnesium, iron and B vitamins, and offers some protein. This would be well-paired with organic wine and tea light candles.

SERVES 3 TO 4

CAKES

3–4 cups (335–445 g) cooked quinoa, as desired

1¼ cups (225 g) purée of your favorite squash, or baked squash or sweet potato

¼ cup (60 ml) lemon juice

1 tsp garlic powder

½ cup (65 g) chickpea flour

¼ cup (20 g) nutritional yeast

1 tsp lemongrass powder

1 tsp turmeric powder

½ tsp smoked paprika powder

Salt and pepper, as desired

Extra extra-virgin olive oil, for cooking

ASPARAGUS

2 tbsp (30 ml) extra-virgin olive oil

1 clove garlic, peeled and finely chopped

1 bunch (1 lb [455 g]) asparagus

1 batch Maple Dijon Dressing (page 239)

½ cup (60 g) chopped pecans

To make the cakes, mix together all the ingredients, except the salt, pepper and oil, by hand or in a food processor until evenly combined into a thick paste. If you'd like more quinoa for its texture and flavor, add another cup (112 g). Add salt and pepper according to your preference.

Heat a nonstick pan on medium-low or low heat with a splash of olive oil. Form the quinoa squash batter into patties/cakes and cook in the pan; around 3 to 5 minutes each side, or until they begin to brown and get crispy. (The first couple cakes will probably be experiments to figure out which heat setting works best, and to heat up the pan evenly.)

For the asparagus, heat the olive oil and garlic in a pan on low heat, and cook the garlic on its own for 1 to 2 minutes. Add the asparagus and cook for 8 to 10 minutes or until tender.

Serve the cakes over the asparagus, topped with Maple Dijon dressing and pecans.

GREEN PEA PATTIES ON BUTTER LETTUCE WITH HORSERADISH DRESSING

This horseradish sauce is zippy and pairs perfectly with the light, juicy lettuce and dense, savory patties. You could add some nice buns here to make this into a burger situation. Peas are high in the antioxidant vitamin A, which is important for eye and skin health. They also provide protein and fiber. Spinach offers vitamin K (helps with blood clotting) and iron (necessary for transporting oxygen where it needs to be!).

SERVES 3 TO 4

PATTIES
2 cups (300 g) peas

2 cups (80 g) spinach

1 cup (170 g) almonds

1 cup (130 g) chickpea flour

½ cup (40 g) nutritional yeast

½ cup (20 g) basil

3 tbsp (45 ml) olive oil

1 tbsp (15 ml) lemon juice

1 tbsp (10 g) garlic powder

1 tbsp (16 g) miso paste

Salt and pepper, as desired

TO SERVE
2–3 heads butter lettuce, washed and chopped

Horseradish Dressing (page 253)

GARNISH
3 tbsp (32 g) slivered almonds (optional)

3 tbsp (28 g) green peas (optional)

To make the patties, put all the ingredients in a food processor and process until you have a semi-chunky, thick batter. You should be able to form it into patties or balls with your hands. If it's too moist, add extra chickpea flour. If it's too dry, add extra water, olive oil or lemon juice.

In a large nonstick pan on medium or medium-low heat, heat up a bit of olive oil. It should be hot enough that when you place in a cake, it immediately begins to sizzle. Form your batter into balls or cakes (I use an ice-cream scoop and then pat them down into patties) and cook on medium-low heat; about 5 minutes for each side. They should hold together and become a dark, crispy brown once done. Depending on your stove, low heat might be sufficient. If you don't have room to cook them all right away, you may need to repeat the process once or twice.*

Serve on beds of fresh butter lettuce, drizzled with the horseradish dressing. Garnish with almonds and peas, if you like.

*Alternatively, bake the cakes for 30 minutes at 400°F (204°C).

BLACK BEAN MEATBALLS WITH SPAGHETTI + ROSEMARY CREAM

My friends were pretty surprised that these "meatballs" were made entirely from plants. But when you think about it, it's not that impossible to believe. Food is just combinations of varying flavors, textures, shapes, smells and colors, so you can recreate or adapt most anything if you pay enough attention to what makes a food special in the first place. It will never be the same, since each food is unique, but you can get pretty close. I think the sautéed onions and garlic go a long way here, adding a rich umami flavor. They also provide powerful antioxidant properties and may help fight cancer and heart disease. The texture of the meatballs is firm and moist, not crumbly or overly dry (like some vegan meatballs tend to be). Beans and tofu add fiber, protein, calcium and iron.

SERVES 3 TO 4

MEATBALLS
2 medium-size onions

2 cloves garlic

2–3 tbsp (30–45 ml) olive oil

2 tbsp (30 ml) lemon juice

1½ cups (258 g) cooked black beans

1 cup (96 g) almond flour

¾ cup (98 g) chickpea flour

⅓ cup (83 g) tofu

⅓ cup (27 g) nutritional yeast

¼ cup (28 g) ground flax seeds

½ tsp chipotle powder

Salt and pepper, as desired

11–14 oz (300–400 g) cooked gluten-free spaghetti

Rosemary Garlic Almond Cream (page 236)

To make the meatballs, mince and then sauté the onions and garlic in the olive oil for 10 minutes, or until softened, translucent and beginning to brown. Stir often to cook them evenly.

Put all the ingredients for the meatballs in a food processor and process until you have a semi-chunky, thick batter. You should be able to form it into patties or balls with your hands. If it's too moist, add extra chickpea flour. If it's too dry, add extra water, olive oil or lemon juice.

Heat up a bit of olive oil in a large nonstick pan on medium or medium-low heat. It should be hot enough that when you place in a cake, it immediately begins to sizzle.

Form your batter into balls or patties (I use an ice-cream scoop) and cook on medium-low heat about 8 to 10 minutes, moving them around so they cook evenly. They should hold together and develop a dark, crispy brown crust once done. Depending on your stove, low heat might be sufficient. If you don't have room to cook them all right away, you may need to repeat the process once or twice.*

Coat your pasta in the cream, as desired, and serve with meatballs on top.

*Alternatively, bake the meatballs for 30 minutes at 400°F (204°C).

SOY-FREE

RAW

QUICK TO MAKE

ZUCCHINI NOODLES WITH DILL CASHEW DRESSING + PINE NUTS

Zucchini noodles are ideal on nights you want a lighter meal. Here they're paired with a rich cashew sauce and crunchy pine nuts. I like to eat this in summer, outdoors. Thanks to its mild flavor, zucchini is a versatile food (in fact it's a fruit, and more specifically, a squash). Thanks to its fiber content, it can help with digestion; it also provides cancer-fighting antioxidant power, potassium and manganese.

SERVES 2 TO 3

NOODLES
3 small zucchinis

2 carrots (optional)

1–2 tbsp (15–30 ml) extra-virgin olive oil (optional)

Pinch of sea salt (optional)

DRESSING
½ cup (55 g) cashews

2 tbsp (30 ml) lime juice

½ cup (120 ml) water, or more as needed

Salt and pepper, as desired

1 tsp dried dill

1 tsp maple syrup

½ tsp garlic powder

TOPPINGS
¼ cup (30 g) pine nuts

2–3 tbsp (4–6 g) edible flowers, dried or fresh

To make the noodles, slice the zucchinis into noodles with a vegetable spiral slicer, cheese grater or vegetable peeler. Place the noodles in a colander or on a paper towel for 20 minutes so they can discard any excess moisture. If you'd like carrot noodles, slice them as well. Coat all the noodles in a little olive oil and salt if you like.

To make the dressing, blend all the ingredients together until smooth. Coat your noodles evenly in the dressing.

Toast the pine nuts lightly if desired! Top your noodles with pine nuts and flowers. This is best enjoyed fresh.

SOY-FREE   RAW

GARDEN LASAGNA WITH ZUCCHINI NOODLES, CASHEW CHEESE, PESTO + HEIRLOOM TOMATO

This recipe is predominantly raw except for the baked sweet potatoes, but you can leave those out if you want. Ideal for a small dinner party, since this will feed a handful of people, but it doesn't keep too well in the fridge. It's wonderful served alongside some protein-rich bean cakes. Using good tomatoes matters; heirlooms from the farmers' market add a heavenly touch. If those aren't available, I'd recommend coating your tomatoes in a bit of olive oil and salt, and roasting for about 20 minutes so they can develop a richer flavor. (Or dehydrate until they begin to smell aromatic and have shrunk a little: this means their flavor has intensified.)

SERVES 3 TO 4

LASAGNA

3 small sweet potatoes

3 small zucchinis

1 tbsp (15 ml) extra-virgin olive oil

Pinch of salt

3 small heirloom tomatoes

2 avocados

1 beet

1 carrot

1 cup (48 g) alfalfa sprouts

Cashew Cheese (page 227)

Walnut Cilantro Pesto (page 248)

GARNISH

¼ cup (20 g) almond slivers

¼ cup (10 g) basil leaves, roughly chopped

If you'd like roasted sweet potatoes, preheat the oven to 350°F (177°C). Cut the sweet potatoes in strips, lengthwise, so you end up with wide, long slices. Bake these for 30 minutes or until they are beginning to brown.

Slice the zucchinis into very thin strips similar to lasagna pasta. I use a mandoline slicer for this. Let the zucchini strips sit on a clean dish towel or in a colander for around 20 minutes so they can discard their excess juice; then coat them in a little olive oil and salt.

Slice the tomatoes and avocados thinly. Shred the beet and carrot.

In a casserole dish, or whatever dish you like, build your lasagna: simply layer all the lasagna ingredients in the order you want. Use as much cheese and pesto as desired; you might have some left over.

Use a sharp knife to cut it into pieces. Garnish with almond slivers and basil leaves. This is best enjoyed fresh.

CREAMY SHIITAKE MUSHROOM PASTA WITH KALE

Mushrooms and greens not only add unique colors, textures and shapes to recipes; they also provide anti-cancer benefits. The coconut milk and flavors from the garlic and ginger create a wonderful balance of sweet and savory notes. Use whatever variety of kale you prefer, and if you can't find shiitake mushrooms, most other varieties will do.

SERVES 2 TO 3

PASTA

2 tbsp (28 g) coconut oil

2 cloves garlic

1 tsp chunk ginger

1 small onion

2 lb (908 g) kale leaves, stems removed

3 cups (175 g) shiitake mushrooms

½ cup (120 ml) full-fat coconut milk, or more as needed

1 tbsp (16 g) miso paste

Spices (such as rosemary, turmeric, chipotle or thyme) (optional)

7–10 oz (200–300 g) gluten-free spaghetti

Olive oil as needed

Salt and pepper, as desired

TOPPINGS

¼ cup (40 g) pumpkin seeds

Dollops of Cashew Cheese (page 227) (optional)

Heat the coconut oil in a medium-size pan on medium or medium-low heat. Mince the garlic, ginger and onion and add to the pan, cooking for 5 to 10 minutes or until aromatic and slightly browning.

Rinse and chop the kale and mushrooms into bite-size pieces. Add the coconut milk, miso and mushrooms to the pan, along with whatever spices you desire. Make sure the miso is evenly incorporated; you might need to whisk it in.

Cook for 10 minutes or until the mushrooms are tender to your liking. Add more coconut milk as needed, when/if it evaporates.

Add the kale and cook for another 5 minutes or so, until the kale is vibrantly green and slightly tender. I prefer mine quite soft.

Boil the spaghetti until al dente, or a couple minutes before you'd usually take it out of the water. Drain and toss it in olive oil and salt.

Add the spaghetti to your pan and cook for an additional 2 to 5 minutes or until the spaghetti has soaked up some of the milk and is cooked to your liking.

Season with salt and pepper as desired. Serve with pumpkin seeds and cheese on top, if you want. This will keep for 3 to 4 days in the fridge.

NAVY BEAN BURGERS WITH VEGGIES + PEANUT SAUCE

I got the idea to serve peanut sauce on a burger from a wonderful restaurant in West Vancouver called Dharma Kitchen. It's kinda genius. Chickpea flour in the burger patties allows them to really firm up once they cool down.

MAKES AROUND 6 TO 8 BURGERS

BURGERS

1 cup (80 g) rolled oats

¾ cup (98 g) chickpea flour

⅓ cup (27 g) nutritional yeast

¼ cup (30 g) walnuts

¼ cup (28 g) ground flax seeds

1 tbsp (10 g) garlic powder

1 tsp dried basil leaves

½ tsp chipotle powder

Salt and pepper, as desired

2 cups (340 g) cooked navy beans

3 tbsp (25 g) shredded beet

3 tbsp (45 ml) olive oil, plus more for cooking

1 tbsp (15 ml) lemon juice

FIXINGS

1 head butter lettuce

2 heirloom tomatoes

1 red onion (optional)

1 avocado

6–8 burger buns

Peanut Sauce (page 235)

To make the burger patties, put all the dry ingredients in a food processor and process until evenly mixed and ground up. Add the remaining ingredients and process until you have a chunky batter that you can shape with your hands. If it's too crumbly, add more beans. If it's too wet, add more oats.

Shape the batter into patties.

In a large nonstick pan on medium or medium-low heat, heat up a bit of olive oil. It should be hot enough that when you place in a burger pattie, it immediately begins to sizzle.

Cook the burgers on medium-low heat, about 5 minutes for each side. They should hold together and become a dark, crispy brown once done. Depending on your stove, low heat might be sufficient. If you don't have room to cook them all right away, you may need to repeat the process once or twice. Let them cool to room temperature for 40 to 60 minutes so they can set and firm up.

Slice the vegetables into thin sections, suitable for serving on burgers. Assemble your burger as desired, adding a big scoop of peanut sauce.

SOURDOUGH BREAD WITH CREAMY EGGPLANT + PESTO

This is definitely a richer meal. It fits the bill on colder winter days when I want something that'll help me feel grounded and warm. Very enjoyable to share with friends and lovers over laid-back conversations in a cozy setting. If you can't find gluten-free sourdough (and/or you don't eat gluten-free), use whatever your fave loaf is instead. Excellent topped with roasted tomatoes.

SERVES 4 TO 5

2 eggplants

Extra-virgin olive oil, as needed

2 tsp (4 g) dried rosemary

Salt and pepper, as desired

1 loaf fresh gluten-free sourdough bread (best from the farmers' market or a local bakery!)

½ batch Walnut Cilantro Pesto (page 248)

3 tbsp (30 g) sesame seeds

Tahini (optional)

Preheat the oven to 400°F (204°C).

Slice the eggplants into ½-inch (1.3-cm) thick disks, so they're like giant coins.

Coat the slices generously and evenly in olive oil, adding the rosemary as well as salt and pepper, as desired.

Bake for 30 minutes. Then flip them over, and continue baking for another 20 to 30 minutes, or until they are melt-in-your-mouth tender and beginning to brown.

If you want, quickly "pan-fry" slices of the sourdough with a tiny bit of olive oil (medium heat in a pan for just a couple minutes each side, or until brown) or toast 'em.

Spread the pesto on your bread slices, and top with eggplant slices. Sprinkle with sesame seeds and a drizzle of tahini if you like. Store the components of this recipe separately for up to a week.

ROASTED POTATOES WITH GARLIC, ROSEMARY + THYME

Roasted potatoes with garlic and herbs is a spiritual experience. On their own they can be a bit rich, so the kale balances that out here. Potatoes are in fact a pretty nutritious food, contrary to popular beliefs. But in any case, feeling emotionally nourished and enjoying comforting food is important for health, regardless of whether the food you're eating is offering a bunch of nutritional benefits or not. I value balance, not binaries.

SERVES 3 TO 4

POTATOES
5 cloves garlic

1 tbsp (3 g) fresh rosemary leaves

½ tbsp (2 g) fresh thyme leaves

4 lb (1.8 kg) Yukon Gold potatoes

3 tbsp (45 ml) extra-virgin olive oil, or more as desired

Salt and pepper, as desired

KALE
2 lb (905 g) curly kale, stems removed

1 tbsp (15 ml) melted coconut oil

1 tsp lemon juice

½–1 tsp flaked salt, as desired

TO SERVE
Spiced Chickpeas (page 232)

½ batch Smoked Paprika Barbecue Sauce (page 243)

¼ cup (30 g) chopped pecans

½ batch Chipotle Cashew Mayo (page 240) (optional)

Preheat the oven to 425°F (218°C).

To prepare the potatoes, first finely chop the garlic and herbs. Wash the potatoes and slice into bite-size pieces. Generously coat them in olive oil, garlic, herbs and salt and pepper.

Bake for 30 to 40 minutes or until the potatoes are brown and crispy around the edges, and tender all the way through (check with a fork).

To prepare the kale, wash and chop it into bite-size pieces. Steam for 8 to 10 minutes or until it's vibrantly green and tender to your liking. Lightly coat in coconut oil, lemon and salt.

Serve the potatoes on a bed of kale with chickpeas, BBQ sauce, pecans and mayo.

SOY-FREE   RAW   QUICK
TO MAKE

CRUNCHY SALAD WITH GINGER SESAME DRESSING

For some unknown reason I tend to favor softer foods, but every now and then I crave a crunch. In those instances, this salad satisfies. It's zesty thanks to the dressing.

SERVES 2

2 heads butter lettuce

3 cups spinach leaves

2 carrots

1 beet, raw

1 green bell pepper

1 apple

¼ cup (60 g) tahini, as desired

Ginger Sesame Dressing
(page 251)

¼ cup (38 g) dried cranberries

¼ cup (30 g) chopped walnuts

¼ cup (40 g) sunflower seeds

Wash, peel, chop and/or shred the produce as needed. I prefer smaller, bite-size pieces, and shredded carrots and beets.

Evenly coat the lettuce and spinach in the dressing, using as much or as little as you want. Add tahini according to your taste and consistency preferences.

Serve in bowls with all the remaining ingredients on top. Best fresh.

NUT-FREE   SOY-FREE

BROCCOLI FRITTATA WITH SUN-DRIED TOMATOES, ONIONS + GARLIC

This is an epic breakfast to share with friends or eat all week. I am in love with this recipe; it's better than the egg-based dishes I remember eating before going vegan. Feel free to experiment with different vegetables in the filling: sautéed or grilled zucchini, carrot, fresh tomato, spinach or kale would all be wonderful in here. I have made so many variations of this recipe at this point, but the first time I tried it I was inspired by Rita Serano's recipe in *Vegan in 7*. Excellent with Cashew Cheese (page 227), or Walnut Cilantro Pesto (page 248).

SERVES 5 TO 6

2 cloves garlic

2 onions

1 medium head broccoli

3 tbsp (45 ml) extra-virgin olive oil

1 tsp dried basil

1 tsp cumin powder

1 tsp turmeric powder

½ tsp madras curry powder

½ tsp smoked paprika powder

2 cups + 2 tbsp (510 ml) water, divided

1 tbsp (15 ml) apple cider vinegar

¼ cup (28 g) sun-dried tomatoes, stored in olive oil

¼ cup (10 g) chopped basil leaves

Salt and pepper, as desired

1 cup (130 g) chickpea flour

2 cups (480 ml) water

⅓ cup (27 g) nutritional yeast

Preheat the oven to 400°F (204°C).

Mince the garlic and onions, and chop the broccoli into small, thin bite-size pieces. In a pan on medium-low heat, heat the olive oil, and then turn down to low. Add the garlic and onions and sauté for 8 to 10 minutes or until they are translucent and beginning to brown. Add the spices and stir for a couple minutes.

Add the broccoli, 2 tablespoons (30 ml) of water and the vinegar, and saute for another 5 to 7 minutes, or until the broccoli is vibrant green and just starting to soften. Stir in the tomatoes and basil and turn off the heat. Add salt and pepper to taste.

In a bowl, whisk together the chickpea flour with 2 cups (480 ml) of water and the nutritional yeast. Stir in your sautéed vegetables evenly, and then pour into a foil-lined pan, you don't want the batter to be more than 2 to 3 inches (2.5 to 3.7 cm) thick.

Bake for 45 to 60 minutes or until the top of the frittata is dark brown and crispy. The cooking time will depend on the size of your pan (a bigger pan will take less time because it will be a thinner frittata).

Let it cool for 20 to 30 minutes; then slice and enjoy. (You can eat it right away if you really want, but it sets nicer once cooled down.) Serve with Cashew Cheese (page 227), or Walnut Cilantro Pesto (page 248). This will keep for 5 to 7 days in the fridge.

ONE-PAN SPICED RICE NOODLE SAUTÉ WITH TAHINI SAUCE

An easy meal on nights I wanna get in some broccoli and anti-cancer spices and veggies but crave something more substantial than a light, steamed bowl. As usual, the vegetables (besides ginger, onions and garlic) are pretty interchangeable here: You could use other cruciferous greens instead of broccoli, and beet instead of carrot.

SERVES 2

7–11 oz (200–300 g) rice noodles

1 tsp chunk ginger

2 onions

2 garlic cloves

1 medium head broccoli

1 carrot

3 tbsp (45 ml) extra-virgin olive oil

½ tsp cayenne powder, as desired

½ tsp turmeric powder

½ tsp black pepper

½ tsp cumin powder

½ tsp coriander powder

1–2 tbsp (15–30 ml) apple cider vinegar, as desired

1–2 tbsp (15–30 ml) tamari, as desired

1 tbsp (15 ml) maple syrup, optional

2–3 tbsp (30–45 ml) water, as needed

¼ cup (60 g) tahini, as desired

Sun-dried tomatoes (optional)

Cilantro, basil and seeds or nuts, for serving

Leave the noodles in a bowl of boiled water for 10 minutes or until softened slightly, but still firmer than you would enjoy them normally.

Mince the ginger, onions and garlic, and chop the broccoli and carrot into thin, bite-size pieces.

Heat the olive oil in a pan on medium-low heat. Add the ginger, garlic and onion and sauté for 8 minutes, or until translucent and beginning to brown.

Add the spices and sauté another 2 minutes.

Add the broccoli and carrot and sauté for another minute; then add the vinegar, tamari and maple syrup. Add water if the mixture is looking dry (it will also help steam the veggies).

Mix in the noodles and cook until the broccoli, carrot and noodles are as cooked as you prefer, and the liquids have been absorbed into the veggies and noodles.

Stir in the tahini and sun-dried tomatoes and turn off the heat. If your tahini is quite chunky and solid, you may need to add some water or lemon juice to make more of a sauce. Adjust the dish according to taste, adding extra salt if you like.

Serve with fresh cilantro, basil and seeds or chopped nuts.

SNACKS

I am a fan of snacks. I prefer to eat smaller bites throughout the day instead of big-deal meals a few times. It's easier on my tummy and it means I can eat a bigger variety of recipes. Hehe. The recipes in this chapter are perfect for keeping yourself energized on the go, light meals on days you aren't so hungry, sides for mains and, well . . . snacks, for whenever you want them! You can make a lot of these more substantial meals by adding rice or quinoa, baked sweet potatoes, avocado toast or a protein, like bean cakes or tofu.

SOY-FREE   RAW   QUICK
TO PREPARE

DOUBLE CHOCOLATE BITES WITH NUT PULP

I make my own nondairy milks at home a lot, so I always end up with a chunk of nut pulp when the milk is done (i.e. what's left after you strain the milk through a fine cloth). I used to simply throw this in the compost, but eventually all that food waste started to bother me so I began incorporating it into my recipes. I usually use the pulp as a base for energy bites or cookies. I am keeping this recipe simple, so feel free to add whatever else you like (ex. vanilla, salt, cinnamon, maca . . .). For my nondairy milk recipes, see page 209.

**MAKES ~12 LARGE OR
~20 SMALL BITES**

BITES
¼ cup (23 g) cashews

1 cup (80 g) rolled oats

1 cup (85 g) nut pulp

¼ cup (60 ml) melted coconut oil, plus more if needed

¼ cup (60 ml) brown rice syrup

3 tbsp (21 g) cacao powder

CHOCOLATE COATING
1.4 oz (40 g) chopped dark chocolate (or dark chocolate chips)

TOPPINGS
1–2 tbsp (11–22 g) slivered almonds

½ tsp flaked salt

To make the bites, grind the cashews and oats into flour in a food processor or blender. Then, by hand or in a food processor, mix together all the ingredients until you have a moist, thick dough that holds its shape. If it's too crumbly, add 1 tablespoon (15 ml) more of coconut oil, or 1 tablespoon (15 ml) of lemon juice. If it's too moist, add 1 to 3 tablespoons (5 to 15 g) of rolled oats or almond flour.

Roll the dough into balls or shape it into cookies or bars. Leave them in the fridge while you melt the chocolate.

To make the coating, melt the chocolate in a double boiler or in a small pot on low heat, about 3 to 4 minutes. Take it off the heat once it liquifies. Dip your bites, cookies or bars into the chocolate, sprinkle with slivered almonds and/or flaked salt and put in the fridge for 1 to 2 hours so they can set.

SOY-FREE

RAW

**QUICK
TO MAKE**

QUICK ALMOND BUTTER COOKIES WITH COCONUT, HEMP + FLAX

These are in the snack chapter—and not the dessert—because they are dense and not very sweet. I have grown to love them, however, because of their toasty, nutty flavor and unusual, spongy texture. I ADORE almond butter and coconut, and these are the ingredients that shine here, plus you get all the added nutrition of hemp and flax seeds (omega 3's, fiber, magnesium and more). Best enjoyed with extra almond butter, vanilla coconut ice cream or chia berry jam. These are perfect for a filling breakfast, midday snack or satisfying dessert if you don't need much sweetness. The recipe is inspired by one in Katy Beskow's cookbook *15 Minute Vegan*.

SERVES 3 TO 6; MAKES 6 COOKIES

¼ cup (28 g) coconut flour, or almond flour

2 tbsp (14 g) ground flax seeds

2 tbsp (20 g) hemp seeds

Pinch of sea salt

¼ cup (45 g) almond butter

⅓ cup (80 ml) Coconut Milk (page 209)

3 tbsp (45 ml) melted coconut oil

1 tsp vanilla extract

1 tsp stevia powder

Maple syrup, to taste (optional)

¼ cup (45 g) dark chocolate chips (or chopped dark chocolate)

Preheat the oven to 400°F (204°C).

Mix together all the dry ingredients, and then stir in the rest, adding the chocolate last. You should have a moist, thick dough that holds its shape.

Shape the dough into cookies or balls (I use a big ice-cream scoop, then my hands) and place them on a lined baking sheet.

Bake for 9 to 12 minutes; 9 minutes will leave them softer, 12 minutes means crunchier, crumblier cookies.

Let them cool for 5 minutes, and then enjoy! These will keep in the fridge for 2 to 3 days.

Alternatively, if you wanna keep these raw, don't bake them! Leave them in the fridge for 2 hours instead. Equally delicious! In fact . . . maybe more so.

NUT-FREE

SOY-FREE

QUICK TO PREPARE

CHOCOLATE PROTEIN BITES

Great for an on-the-go bite before or after exercise—or anytime—plus, they simultaneously fulfill my chocolate cravings (which are a daily occurrence that I always make sure to honor, in one way or another). Protein is necessary for muscle maintenance and growth, and helps you feel satisfied and full for longer. Chickpeas, flax, hemp and tahini are good sources of protein, iron and fiber.

SERVES 12; MAKES 12 BITES

PROTEIN BITES
⅓ cup (37 g) coconut flour

⅓ cup (85 g) chickpeas

3 tbsp (21 g) ground flax seeds

¼ cup (40 g) hemp seeds

¼ cup (38 g) vegan chocolate flavored protein powder

3 tbsp (45 ml) melted coconut oil

¼ cup (60 g) tahini

Stevia powder or brown rice syrup, as needed (optional)*

COATING
2 tbsp (14 g) cacao powder

Blend together all the ingredients for the protein bites in a food processor until you have a thick dough that can hold its shape when pressed between your fingers. If it's too wet, add rolled oats or more coconut flour. If it's too dry, add more tahini or maple syrup.

Shape the dough into balls, roll in the cacao powder and leave in the fridge for 2 hours to set. Enjoy whenever! These will keep in the fridge for 2 weeks.

*If your protein powder isn't sweetened, you may want to add some sweetener of your own. For this recipe, I use a protein powder that has stevia added.

SOY-FREE   RAW   QUICK
TO MAKE

CINNAMON CHIA PUDDING WITH RASPBERRIES + CHOCOLATE SAUCE

I make a version of this for breakfast every morning. It's consistently a motivator to get my butt outta bed and into the kitchen, because it tastes delicious and provides a light, sustained energy to get the day started. There are endless options for toppings: like cacao nibs with sliced banana, dried cranberries with shredded coconut, chopped dark chocolate with blueberries. . . . In this recipe, we're doin' raspberries with chocolate sauce. Chia pudding is especially excellent when made with fresh almond milk, or any other homemade nondairy milk, and I find DIY milks bind with the chia seeds better than store bought varieties. You are welcome to make the recipe in larger batches for the week (I would suggest storing them in single serving jars or glassware), but I enjoy the morning ritual aspect of making it daily.

SERVES 1 TO 2

CHIA PUDDING
1 cup (240 ml) nondairy milk (page 209)

2 tbsp (20 g) chia seeds

1 tbsp (7 g) ground flax seeds

Scant ¼ cup (20 g) rolled oats

1 tbsp (9 g) raisins (or pitted, chopped dates)

½ tsp cinnamon powder

CHOCOLATE SAUCE
1 tbsp (15 ml) maple syrup

1 tbsp (15 ml) nondairy milk (page 209)

1 heaping tbsp (7 g) cacao powder

Pinch of sea salt

TOPPING
⅓ cup (43 g) raspberries

To make the chia pudding, pour the milk into a bowl and then thoroughly stir all the ingredients together except the cinnamon, which we'll be using later. Leave it in the fridge for 30 minutes. The chia seeds should thicken the whole mixture into a consistency similar to rice pudding. If it doesn't get thick enough, add 1 tablespoon (10 g) more of chia, oats or flax. If it gets too thick, add 2 to 3 tablespoons (30 to 45 ml) of nondairy milk. If you have the time, let it sit overnight and add more milk the next morning.

To make the chocolate sauce, stir or whisk together the ingredients until smooth. If it's too runny, add 1 tablespoon (7 g) more of cacao powder.

Drizzle the chocolate sauce over your pudding and top with berries and extra seeds or chopped nuts, if you like. Sprinkle on the cinnamon and enjoy!

VANILLA CINNAMON DONUT HOLES

In the country I live in, known as Canada to some—and Turtle Island to many others—we have a coffee and donut chain called Tim Horton's. This company offers a well-known, well-loved menu item called Tim Bits; it's basically just donut holes with a branded name. I had to explain all that before I could say: this recipe is inspired by Tim Bits.

MAKES 12 MEDIUM-LARGE DONUT HOLES

DONUT HOLES
¾ cup (60 g) quick oats
1 cup (110 g) cashews
¼ cup (43 g) pitted dates
1 tsp vanilla extract
1 tbsp (15 ml) melted coconut oil
1 tbsp (15 ml) brown rice syrup
1 tbsp (15 ml) water
½ tsp cinnamon powder
⅛ tsp stevia powder
Pinch of sea salt

CINNAMON MAPLE GLAZE
2 tbsp (30 ml) maple syrup
1 tbsp (15 ml) melted coconut oil
½ tsp vanilla extract
1 tsp cinnamon powder

To make the donut holes, place all the ingredients in a food processor and process until you have a moist, semi-crumbly dough. It should hold together when pressed between your fingers. Roll the dough into balls and leave in the freezer for 20 minutes, or until they're solid and cold.

To make the glaze, whisk the ingredients together until you have a smooth mixture.

Coat the chilled donut holes in the glaze and put them back in the freezer for 20 minutes, or until the glaze has hardened. Repeat until you use up all the glaze.

These will keep for 2 weeks in the fridge.

SOY-FREE **RAW** **QUICK TO MAKE**

DARK CHOCOLATE ALMOND BUTTER FUDGE

This fudge is inspired by my friend, Alix, with whom I had the privilege of staying for a few nights in Berlin. Her morning routine always involved roasted almond butter paired with gooey Medjool dates and a few pieces of extra dark chocolate, as well as a creamy bowl of overnight chia pudding. Everyday I looked forward to our breakfast, which she generously shared with me. The date-chocolate-almond butter combo is one I cherish to this day, and since my stay I've fallen in love with 99% dark chocolate. XO to you, Alix!

MAKES 16 SQUARES

3.5 oz (100 g or 1 bar) very dark chocolate, melted

½ cup (90 g) almond butter

½ cup (85 g) pitted dates

In a high-speed blender or small food processor, blend the ingredients until smooth. The mixture will be very thick. If it is too thick for your machine, add almond milk, brown rice syrup, water or more almond butter as needed.

Spread it evenly into a lined pan and leave in the freezer for 20 minutes or until it has hardened.

Slice it into squares and enjoy! Add extra almond butter on top if desired. These will keep for a month in the fridge.

NUT-FREE **SOY-FREE** **RAW** **QUICK TO MAKE**

AVO-CACAO PUDDING

I used to get way too excited about those plastic chocolate pudding cups. Now I can enjoy that same satisfying, creamy, whipped, sweet experience without the refined ingredients or dairy. While the avocado flavor and color is subtle here, it does come through a little bit. If you don't like that, add more dates and cacao powder to mask it.

SERVES 2; MAKES ~2 CUPS

1 avocado

1 tbsp (15 ml) melted coconut oil

½ tsp vanilla powder

Pinch of sea salt

2–3 heaping tbsp (14–21 g) cacao powder, as desired

1 tsp reishi mushroom powder

4 pitted dates, or as desired

¾ cup (180 ml) Coconut Milk (page 209), or more as needed

1 tbsp (15 ml) brown rice syrup (optional)

Blend all the ingredients until smooth and thick. If it's too thick, add more milk, or add milk as desired to get the consistency you prefer. Adjust according to taste, adding more sweetener if desired.

This pudding is best enjoyed right away, ideally with banana slices, berries and Pure Chocolate (page 223).

Alternatively, scoop the pudding into a jar and throw it in the freezer for ice cream later. Don't fill the jar up all the way, or else the glass will crack! Before enjoying, let it thaw for a few minutes (unless you're one of those who prefers really hard ice cream).

SOY-FREE **RAW** **QUICK TO MAKE**

COCO YOGURT BOWL WITH JAM + COOKIES

I don't know why I love yogurt so much, but here I am. Here, the deep rich flavor of fermented coconut cream pairs perfectly with the light, tart sweetness of fresh berry jam. For texture and substance, oatmeal cookies round off the bowl for a filling and sweet snack, dessert or small meal. We've got healthy fats in here, as well as probiotics and antioxidants. If you want more crunch, do add a handful of Coconut Cranberry Granola (page 156).

SERVES 1

½ cup (123 g) Easy Coconut Yogurt (page 215)

2 tbsp (40 g) Tayberry Jam (page 179)

1 Nutty Oatmeal Cookie (page 139)

1 sliced banana

OPTIONAL ADD-INS
1 tbsp (15 ml) maple syrup

¼ cup (38 g) berries

1 tbsp (5 g) coconut flakes

1 tbsp (10 g) hemp seeds

¼ cup (31 g) Coconut Cranberry Granola (page 156)

Scoop the yogurt into a bowl and add the jam, cookie and banana slices.

Add the extras if desired! Eat it right away.

NUT-FREE SOY-FREE RAW QUICK TO MAKE

SIMPLEST SESAME FUDGE

This is a favorite snack of mine, and it's ready in literal seconds. If you know anything about me, you know of my undying love for tahini. I buy mine from Middle Eastern and north African groceries in my neighborhood because it tastes the best and is so creamy that you can easily pour or drizzle it over your food. The tahini I have previously bought from Western companies simply does not compare (and it's more expensive). In this recipe—which could not be any simpler—we get all the fudgy, sweet, gooey magic of Medjool dates mixed with the creamy, salty, roasted notes of tahini. I like adding whole sesame seeds for a crunch. The flavors here are reminiscent of halva (translating to "sweet/candy"), a delicious and popular recipe usually made from sugar and tahini, originating in the Middle East and Mediterranean but enjoyed across Asia, Europe and the globe.

SERVES 1

2 big, gooey, pitted Medjool dates

1 tbsp (15 g) tahini

1 tsp sesame seeds (optional)

Scoop the tahini into the center of the dates, sprinkle with sesame seeds and enjoy.

SOY-FREE   RAW   QUICK
                   TO PREPARE

NUTTY OATMEAL COOKIES WITH FLAX + HEMP

I love chewy oatmeal raisin cookies, so here's my unbaked and gluten-free version! I enjoy these on their own for a quick snack, or with Easy Coconut Yogurt (page 215) and banana slices in the morning. I have to thank Laura Wright, author of *The First Mess Cookbook*, for giving me the idea, in a raw cookie recipe of hers, to add lemon juice to raw treats; it lightens up the whole flavor profile.

**SERVES 8 TO 16; MAKES
8 LARGE COOKIES**

½ cup (85 g) almonds

½ cup (76 g) Brazil nuts

1 cup (80 g) rolled oats

Pinch of sea salt

¾ tsp cinnamon powder

¾ tsp vanilla extract

1 tbsp (15 ml) lemon juice

1 cup (170 g) pitted dates

2 tbsp (14 g) ground flax seeds

2 tbsp (14 g) cacao powder
(optional)

1 tbsp (15 ml) maple syrup
(optional)

¼ cup (40 g) hemp seeds

¼ cup (38 g) raisins

Grind the almonds, Brazil nuts and oats into flour in a blender or food processor.

In a food processor, add your flour and the rest of the ingredients—except the hemp seeds, raisins, maple syrup and cacao—and process until you have a thick, moist dough.

If you want chocolate cookies, add the cacao. If you'd like them sweeter, add the maple syrup. Add the hemp seeds and raisins and process quickly one last time to get them evenly incorporated, or mix them in by hand. The dough should hold its shape when pressed between your fingers. If it's too crumbly, add a splash of water or coconut oil. If it's too moist, add extra hemp seeds.

Shape the dough into cookies, bars or balls and leave in the fridge for 30 to 60 minutes, or until they have hardened up a bit. These will keep for up to 2 weeks in the fridge.

SOY-FREE   RAW   QUICK
TO PREPARE

DOUBLE CHOCOLATE HEMP PROTEIN BARS

Hemp seeds are a great source of healthy fats, fiber, essential fatty acids, vitamin E and protein. In fact, about 25 percent of hemp seeds' calories are from protein. Hemp seeds contain acids that can help with PMS, and skin problems like eczema, and their fiber content can aid digestion. They have a distinctly nutty flavor that I personally like, though it may take some getting used to for some folks. These bars are basically rich double chocolate cookies, with the added benefits of this wonderful seed. PS: No, hemp will NOT get you high. Sorry.

MAKES 16 BARS

BARS
1 cup (116 g) walnuts
½ cup (40 g) rolled oats
¼ cup + 2 tbsp (42 g) hemp protein powder
1 cup (170 g) pitted dates
¼ cup (38 g) raisins
½ tsp vanilla powder
Pinch of sea salt
2 tbsp (14 g) cacao powder
1 tbsp (14 g) coconut oil
1–2 tbsp (15–30 ml) water, as needed
1 tbsp (15 ml) brown rice syrup
2–3 tbsp (20–30 g) hemp seeds, for topping

CHOCOLATE COATING
1 batch Pure Chocolate (page 223)

To make the bars, in a food processor, process all the ingredients except the hemp seeds into a thick, moist dough. It should hold its shape when pressed between two fingers. If it's too crumbly, add 1 to 2 tablespoons (15 to 30 ml) of water. If it's too moist, add more hemp powder.

Press the dough into a lined pan.

Now you can pour the chocolate over the top of this, sprinkle it with 2 to 3 tablespoons (20 to 30 g) of hemp seeds and leave it in the fridge to set for at least 1 hour (you won't need as much chocolate for this method). Or you can leave the dough in the fridge until it has hardened up a bit, slice it into bars and then coat each individual bar with chocolate and hemp seeds. Up to you! These will keep for 2 weeks in the fridge.

SOY-FREE   RAW

DATE SQUARES WITH COCONUT ALMOND CRUST

The base of these squares reminds me of sugar cookies. . . . I think it's because of the unique texture of almond pulp. Thanks to the walnuts, dates, coconut and oats, these are an energizing, naturally sweet treat to keep your body and brain happy. For a quick and easy dessert-like breakfast or snack, I'd suggest pairing one of these with a rich mug of Dandy Blend tea.

SERVES 9 TO 16; MAKES 9 LARGE SQUARES

BASE

1 cup (80 g) rolled oats

1 cup (85 g) almond pulp (leftover from making Almond–Brazil Nut Milk, page 210)

1 tbsp (14 g) coconut oil

1 cup (75 g) coconut flakes

¼ cup (48 g) coconut sugar

¼ cup (28 g) ground flax seeds

Pinch of sea salt

DATE PASTE

2 cups (340 g) pitted dates

⅔ cup (160 g) coconut milk, or more as needed

2 tbsp (30 g) coconut oil

1 tsp lemon juice

1 tsp vanilla extract

⅛ tsp sea salt

⅛ tsp cinnamon powder

⅛ tsp nutmeg powder

⅛ tsp ginger powder

CRUST

½ cup (58 g) walnuts

½ cup (38 g) coconut flakes

½ cup (48 g) almond flour

¼ cup (20 g) rolled oats

1 tbsp (15 ml) maple syrup

1 tbsp (14 g) coconut oil

To make the base, process all the ingredients together in a food processor until you have a moist dough. It should hold its shape when pressed between your fingers. Press it into the bottom of a lined pan and leave in the fridge.

To make the date paste, blend or process all the ingredients together until smooth, adding coconut milk as needed to get a thick, smooth consistency. Spread it onto your base and place it back in the fridge.

To make the crust, process the ingredients in a food processor for just a few seconds to chop up the walnuts and get everything evenly mixed. You want it to remain chunky though. Press it evenly onto your date paste layer and leave it in the fridge for at least 3 hours, or overnight, to set.

Slice and enjoy! These will keep for 2 weeks in the fridge.

SOY-FREE RAW QUICK
TO PREPARE

TWO-INGREDIENT PEANUT BUTTER ENERGY BARS

These are inspired by Larabars: those delicious, chewy energy bars you can get at health food stores and gas stations alike. It would be a challenge to make them any simpler or more delicious. This recipe reminds me of peanut butter fudge. The amount of dates you'll need to use will depend on the gooeyness of your dates: the less gooey, the more you'll need. Instead of bars, you could alternatively roll these into balls and enjoy on oatmeal, coated in chocolate, with ice cream or solo. Endless options abound.

MAKES 12 TO 15 BARS

1 cup (180 g) crunchy peanut butter

2–3 cups (340–510 g) pitted dates, as needed

2 tbsp (14 g) ground flax seeds (optional)

⅛ tsp sea salt (optional)

ADD-INS
Cinnamon

Vanilla

Ginger

Chocolate chips

Hemp seeds

Throw both the ingredients in a food processor and process until you have a very thick dough. If it's too moist and your food processor can't handle it, add flax seeds and/or more dates to loosen up the dough. Add sea salt if desired. Feel free to add other flavorings like cinnamon, vanilla, ginger, chocolate chips, hemp seeds, etc.

Press the dough firmly into a lined pan and leave it in the fridge for at least 2 hours; then slice it into bars and store in the fridge for up to a month.

Note: Use whatever nut butter you like!

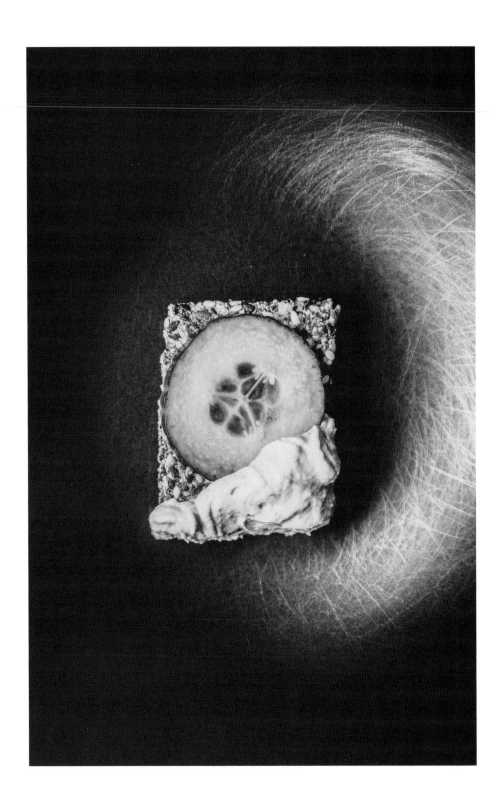

SOY-FREE   RAW

CHEESE 'N' CRACKERS

Perfect for parties or get-togethers, this savory, salty, creamy, crunchy, garlicky, herby combo is difficult to stop eating. But then again, you don't have to stop eating if you don't want to! So it's all good.

SERVES 15 TO 20 OR SAVE TO SNACK ON AS DESIRED

2 batches Seedy Herby Crackers (page 231)

1 batch Cashew Cheese with Garlic + Herbes de Provence (page 227)

Sliced fruits and vegetables (such as cucumber, tomato, avocado, carrot, apple, fig)

Create your own cheese platter! Arrange the crackers, cheese and sliced veg/fruit on a tray or board, and serve.

Alternatively, store the cheese, crackers and sliced fruit/veg in your fridge and snack on it whenever you like.

SOY-FREE RAW QUICK TO MAKE

ALMOND BUTTER CUPS

I find a lot of foods sexy, and almond butter cups are one of those foods. They are such a luxurious, unapologetic and elegant item, which I cannot help but admire and desire on a weekly basis. In this version, raw chocolate offers iron and antioxidant power; and almond butter provides protein, vitamin E and fiber. These are a sacred snack, energy-booster, pre-workout bite or dessert that I am always grateful for.

MAKES ~12 MEDIUM CUPS; 6 LARGE; 24 SMALL

1 batch Pure Chocolate (page 223), in liquid form

1 cup (250 g) almond butter, as needed

Using half the chocolate, pour a little into the bottoms of cupcake papers, lined tart molds or chocolate molds. Use as many as needed until you've used half the chocolate. Put them in the freezer for 5 to 10 minutes, or until the chocolate had solidified.

Spoon a dollop of almond butter into each of the cups or molds. Use as much or as little almond butter as you prefer or need. Pour the remaining chocolate over this and put it back in the freezer for 10 minutes or until solid.

Enjoy! These will keep in the fridge or freezer for up to a month, but will probably disappear faster than that.

NUT-FREE **SOY-FREE** **QUICK TO MAKE**

HUMMUS 'N' VEG BOARD

This is ideal snacking material for one person all week or to serve at a little party. Bell peppers are suuuuper high in cancer-fighting vitamin C and antioxidants (as are carrots), cucumbers and celery are hydrating for the skin thanks to their water content, and the crackers provide gut-healthy fiber and essential fatty acids. Hummus itself is a pretty magical food rich in fiber, iron and protein—thanks to chickpeas and tahini—to keep you full and satisfied for longer.

SERVES 5 TO 6

1 cucumber

2 carrots

3 celery stalks

1 red bell pepper

1 yellow bell pepper

1 cup (180 g) olives, and other fave pickled foods

Crackers (page 228 or page 231) or flatbread/pita bread

1 batch Hummus (page 254)

Wash and chop the produce as needed. I'd recommend cutting the veg so they're in long, bite-size pieces suited for scooping up hummus.

If you're making this for a party, arrange the veg on a platter or board alongside the olives, crackers/bread and bowl of hummus. If you're food prepping for the week, store everything in containers in the fridge.

This will all keep for 1 week in the fridge.

SOY-FREE

QUICK TO MAKE

GOOD OLE OATS WITH A BUNCH OF GOOD STUFF ON TOP

My original comfort food, spruced waaay up. I know a lot of people associate oatmeal with sad, pale mush (and in many cases this is super valid), but as a kid I always looked forward to the stuff. Probably because I covered it with big spoonfuls of brown sugar. No matter your history with oats, they provide a great amount of fiber, which can help control blood sugar levels and has been shown to lower bad cholesterol as well as protect heart health. When you top them with rich ingredients like dark chocolate and almond butter, it's like you're eating a bowl of warm cookie dough. No down sides. (Unless you dislike cookie dough . . . ?!)

SERVES 1 TO 2

OATS
½ cup (40 g) rolled oats

1 cup (240 ml) cold water

Pinch of sea salt

TOPPINGS
3 tbsp (25 g) chopped Pure Chocolate (page 223)

2 tbsp (32 g) almond butter

1 sliced banana

1 cup (152 g) berries

1 tbsp (11 g) almond slivers

2 tbsp (30 ml) coconut sugar or maple syrup

To make the oatmeal, first throw the oats in the cold water with a pinch of salt. Bring it to a boil, stirring occasionally with a wooden spurtle or spoon.

Once boiling, turn the heat to low (still stirring occasionally) until the oats are the consistency you like, this will take a few minutes. I like mine thick, and then I add nondairy milk to thin it out and cool it down so I can eat it right away.

Top it with all the fixings and whatever else your lovely heart desires. Enjoy right away.

NUT-FREE

SOY-FREE

RAW

QUICK TO MAKE

SPIRULINA CHOCOLATE

All the elegance of dark chocolate plus the benefits of spirulina. I genuinely enjoy this flavor combination, but it might be an acquired taste for some people. I'd highly recommend snacking on this with almond butter and dates.

MAKES 3 CHOCOLATE BARS; 1½ CUPS (270 G)

1 batch Pure Chocolate (page 223)

2–3 tbsp (14–21 g) spirulina powder

If you have just made the chocolate and it's still in liquid form, simply whisk in the spirulina powder, according to taste, until evenly incorporated. Otherwise, remelt the chocolate and follow the same step.

Pour it into chocolate molds, or onto a plate lined with parchment paper or plastic wrap, and leave in the freezer for 20 minutes or until it has solidified.

Store in the fridge for up to a month.

SOY-FREE QUICK TO MAKE

COCONUT CRANBERRY GRANOLA WITH WALNUTS

I eat a lot of this before it gets to the oven. It's excellent with yogurt and sliced fruit, or over coconut ice cream. Cacao nibs are rich in antioxidants, iron, copper, manganese, magnesium and fiber; they also contain a bit of caffeine, so this is a great breakfast recipe. Walnuts are terrific for the brain and heart, providing antioxidants, omega-3 fatty acids and polyunsaturated fats.

SERVES 16; MAKES ~8 CUPS (885 G)

2 cups (232 g) roughly chopped walnuts

2 cups (150 g) coconut flakes

2 cups (160 g) rolled oats

1 cup (128 g) sunflower seeds

1 cup (100 g) cacao nibs

1 cup (150 g) dried cranberries

½ tsp sea salt

½–1 cup (118–240 ml) coconut nectar, as desired

1 tsp vanilla extract

Preheat the oven to 300°F (150°C).

Mix together all the dry ingredients evenly, and then stir in the coconut nectar and vanilla until evenly coated. Adjust according to taste; it should be a bit sweeter than you'd normally want at this point (it will mellow out once toasted), but should taste really yummy.

Toast for 15 minutes on a lined baking sheet, and then mix everything up. Toast for another 10 to 15 minutes, or until the granola smells fragrant and is beginning to brown. The longer you let it toast, the crunchier it will be.

Let it cool and enjoy! This can be stored at room temperature or in the fridge for up to a month.

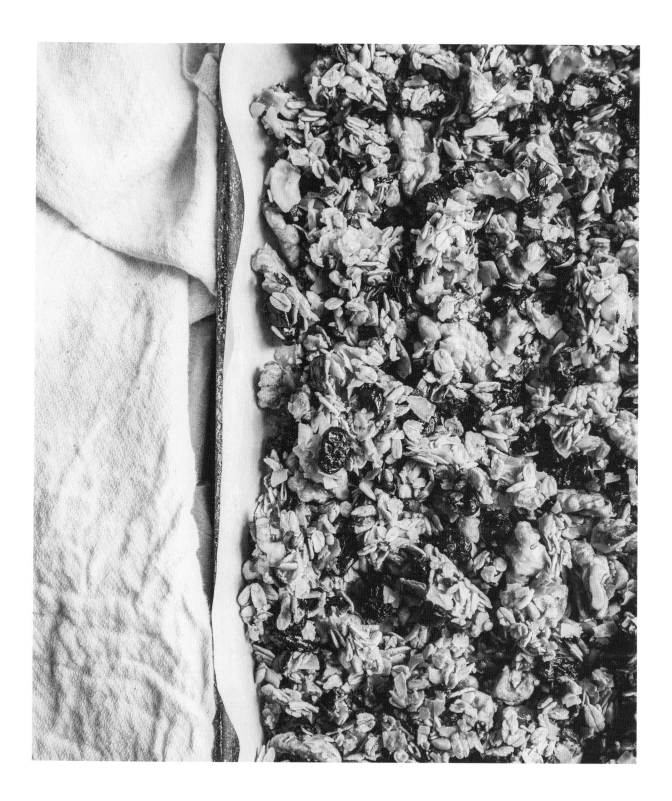

SATISFYING SWEETS

This is my fave category of food, to be honest. I'm an eat-dessert-first type person, or ideally, eat-dessert-first-second-and-third. If I consumed a lot of refined sweets, my high intake of them might make me feel weird. But thankfully I don't have to worry about that, because wholesome, vegan desserts are bountiful in this (occasionally) generous world! They provide me with vitamins, minerals and nutrients, fiber and healthy fats, all while tasting just as yummy as their non-vegan counterparts. Don't limit what ya love! Don't skip dessert!

These recipes are light on refined sweeteners. Sometimes I use coconut sugar, brown rice syrup and maple syrup because they just taste so damn great, but for the most part I prefer stevia, dates and other dried and fresh fruit. For fats, I like using whole nuts and seeds, their butters, and coconut oil and cacao butter.

LUSCIOUS PUMPKIN PIE WITH CRANBERRIES + WHIPPED CREAM

Here's one of my favorite recipes ever, and the best part is: the batter is perfect as a pudding when you don't have the patience to wait for the pie to set. I have made many variations of this recipe (another is on my blog!) and the original was inspired by one in *The Greenhouse Cookbook* by Emma Knight with Hana James, Deeva Green and Lee Reitelman. You could also turn these into tarts. Even though pumpkin pie is a recipe usually reserved for cooler months, I enjoy this year-round. If you'd like it strictly raw, you can make your own pumpkin purée . . . it's just a bit of a hassle.

SERVES 9 TO 12

CRUST

½ cup (60 g) walnuts

½ cup (40 g) rolled oats

½ cup (85 g) pitted dates

1 tsp vanilla extract

Pinch of sea salt

2 tbsp (14 g) ground flax seeds

1–2 tsp (5–10 ml) water, if needed

To make the crust, grind the walnuts and oats into flour in a food processor. Add the dates and process until they're broken down. Add the rest of the ingredients and process until the dough is slightly sticky, crumbly and can hold its shape when pressed between two fingers. If it's too crumbly, add a little water. If it's too moist, add extra flax seeds or oats.

Press evenly into the bottom of a pie dish or springform pan, and leave it in the fridge.

(continued)

LUSCIOUS PUMPKIN PIE WITH CRANBERRIES + WHIPPED CREAM (CONTINUED)

FILLING

1¾ cups (415 g) pumpkin purée

¼ cup (60 ml) melted cacao butter

2 tbsp (30 ml) melted Coconut Butter (page 212)

¼ cup (60 ml) full-fat canned coconut milk

1 tsp vanilla extract

Pinch of sea salt

¼ cup (38 g) dried cranberries

¼ cup (22 g) dried goji berries

¼ cup (60 ml) brown rice syrup

1 tbsp (15 ml) lemon juice

1½ tsp (4 g) cinnamon powder

½ tsp ginger powder

¼ tsp ground cloves

¼ tsp ground nutmeg

⅛ tsp ground cardamom

SALTED CARAMEL

2 tbsp (30 g) melted coconut oil

1 tbsp (15 ml) brown rice syrup

1 tbsp (15 ml) maple syrup

1 tbsp (15 ml) water

¼ tsp sea salt

⅛ tsp vanilla powder

Whipped Coconut Cream (page 206)

To make the filling, blend all the ingredients until smooth and delicious. Adjust the spices and sweetener according to taste.

Pour it evenly over your crust and let it set in the fridge overnight or for at least 5 hours, otherwise it'll be more like pudding (which isn't necessarily a bad thing).

To make the caramel, stir together the ingredients until you have a sweet, salty, drizzly mixture.

Spread the whipped cream over your pie. Drizzle the caramel over your pie. Slice and enjoy! This will keep in the fridge for 2 weeks (the flavors get richer over time) and in the freezer for a month.

DARK 'N' DENSE CHOCOLATE CAKE

This is everything I crave in a slice of choco cake: it's dense, moist, satisfying and served with lots of frosting. It's not super sweet, but I prefer my treats that way because it means I can eat more of them without feeling wonky. This cake is made from oats, black beans, coconut milk and dates. All these foods have loads of benefits, from improving digestion to protecting heart and blood health. I guess you could call it chocolate cake with benefits. Eyyy! This would be a lovely recipe to pair with a light, tart berry sauce. The cake recipe also makes amazing brownies, and the frosting recipe makes a terrific mousse.

SERVES 12 TO 18; MAKES 1 LARGE CAKE

CAKE

1 cup (80 g) rolled oats

1 (13.5-oz [400-ml]) can coconut milk

1 (15-oz [425-g]) can black beans

1½ cups (255 g) pitted dates

2 heaping tbsp (14 g) cacao powder

1 tsp baking soda

1 tsp vanilla extract

½ tsp sea salt

¼ cup (60 ml) nondairy milk (page 209), if needed

Preheat the oven to 350°F (177°C). Line a cake or bread pan with parchment paper, or grease with coconut oil.

To start making the cake, in a high-speed blender, grind the oats into flour.

Add the rest of the ingredients and blend until you have a smooth, thick cake batter. It should be slightly thinner than the consistency of yogurt. If it's too thick for your blender to handle, add a little nondairy milk to keep things moving.

Adjust according to taste, adding more sweetener or cacao if desired.

Pour it into a lined cake or bread pan and bake for 35 to 40 minutes, or until a fork stuck in the middle of the pan comes out clean.

(continued)

DARK 'N' DENSE CHOCOLATE CAKE (CONTINUED)

FROSTING

1 cup (240 ml) Coconut Milk (page 209), or more as needed

¼ cup (43 g) pitted dates

½ cup (55 g) cashews

½ cup (85 g) hazelnuts

⅓ cup (80 ml) brown rice syrup

⅛ tsp sea salt

2 tbsp (14 g) cacao powder

⅓ cup (75 g) cacao butter wafers, melted

1 tbsp (15 ml) melted coconut oil

TOPPINGS

Toasted coconut flakes

Pure Chocolate (page 223), melted

To make the frosting, blend all the ingredients until smooth. If it's too thick, add a little more coconut milk. Leave the frosting in the fridge overnight so it can thicken up. If you don't wanna wait that long, at least give it a few hours, and spread it more thinly on a plate in the fridge so it solidifies faster.

Slice your cake into layers, frost each and then re-layer. Slice and enjoy! These will keep for a week in the fridge, but I'm sure they'll disappear much faster.

Optional: Sprinkle on some lightly toasted coconut flakes for a crunch, and drizzle on chocolate sauce!

Note: If you do want the recipe sweeter, add ¼ cup (60 ml) of maple syrup to the batter, as well as the frosting.

NUT-FREE   SOY-FREE   RAW   QUICK
                                      TO PREPARE

PINEAPPLE, RASPBERRY + CHERRY SORBET

This recipe is inspired by a stevia-sweetened raspberry sorbet I've gotten a couple times at my city's Sunday farmers' market. Normally I am *not* stevia's #1 fan, but somehow it works perfectly here when paired with sweet, frozen fruit and a bit of sour, juicy citrus (in this case, lime). I eat this recipe and countless variations of it all summer; it's idyllic on those too-hot evenings in the peak of the season when I can't be bothered to cook or consume a hot, dense meal.

SERVES 1 TO 2

SORBET
¾ cup (185 g) frozen pineapple chunks
¾ cup (95 g) frozen raspberries
½ cup (78 g) frozen cherries
1 tsp maca powder
1 tsp lucuma powder
1 peeled, chopped lime
⅛ tsp stevia powder (optional)

TOPPINGS
¼ cup (30 g) raspberries
¼ cup (45 g) cherries

Blend all the ingredients together in a high-speed blender until smooth and thick, just like . . . sorbet! It will take a couple minutes, and your blender may need to take breaks if you think it's being overworked. You will need a tamper to keep pushing the ingredients toward the blender blades, or else turn off the blender periodically and push everything down with a spoon. Do NOT use a spoon while the blender is on!

Scoop into a bowl, or bowls, and top with fresh berries and cherries.

FUDGY DARK CHOCOLATE WITH TAHINI

Chocolate is my lifeblood. I eat it every day and it brings me a deep, meaningful joy. I am not, however, talking about chocolate candy bars from the corner store. I am talking about *dark* chocolate infused with good stuff like nuts, seeds, berries, coconut and superfoods—in this recipe: chaga and reishi mushrooms, but don't worry, you can't taste 'em—and sweetened with maple or coconut sugar. Cacao products are similar to cocoa products, but they've simply been processed at lower temperatures and so are said to be more nutritious. Use either, as you like. The flavor profiles are quite different so I enjoy both depending on how I am feeling. Cacao is spicier, sharper and more floral; while cocoa tastes more robust, rounded, roasted and reminds me of coffee or chocolate cake. Buying ethically produced cacao or cocoa products matters, so please do when they're available. Check out the Food Empowerment Project for more info on Fair Trade–Certified™ chocolate brands. I am vegan for the justice of animals, but it goes beyond that: I want the foods I eat to be fair for everyone involved, including the workers who grow and pick them.

SERVES ~16

FUDGY CHOCOLATE

⅓ cup (75 g) cacao butter wafers

⅓ cup (80 ml) coconut oil

¼ cup (60 ml) brown rice syrup

1 tsp vanilla powder

¾ cup (85 g) cacao powder

⅛ tsp sea salt

2 tbsp (30 g) tahini

1 tsp reishi mushroom powder

1 tsp chaga mushroom powder

3–4 tbsp (45–60 ml) nondairy milk (page 209), if needed

TOPPINGS

¼ cup (28 g) slivered almonds

½ tsp flaked salt

In a medium pot, melt the cacao butter and coconut oil on low heat.

Whisk in the brown rice syrup until it's thoroughly incorporated.

Stir or whisk in the rest of the ingredients until smooth and delicious, like a thick chocolate sauce. If the mixture is too thick, add almond milk in small increments. If you need more sweetener, add 1 to 2 tablespoons (15 to 30 ml) more of brown rice syrup.

Pour into a pan lined with saran wrap or parchment paper, sprinkle with almonds or flaked salt and leave in the fridge until it has set (around 2 hours).

NUT-FREE   SOY-FREE   RAW   QUICK TO MAKE

MATCHA GINGER ICE CREAM

Green tea ice cream is a popular treat in Japan, balancing sweet and bitter notes in frozen lusciousness. Here I have developed my own version using bananas, zucchini and coconut. Honestly, that doesn't sound great, but it ends up quite delicious. I promise you cannot taste the zucchini, but if you don't trust me, you can just leave it out. I like the addition of ginger for a zing towards the end of the flavor profile.

SERVES 1 TO 2

2 frozen, chopped bananas

⅓ cup (46 g) frozen zucchini chunks

¼ tsp vanilla extract

Pinch of stevia powder

½–1 tsp matcha powder

2 tbsp (30 ml) Ginger Syrup (page 219)

3 tbsp (45 ml) full-fat coconut milk, as needed

Blend all the ingredients until smooth, like soft serve. Add matcha and syrup according to taste, and add coconut milk as needed or desired to get the consistency you want. If you don't have/want to use ginger syrup, you can substitute brown rice syrup along with a ¼ teaspoon of ginger powder.

Enjoy immediately, or throw it in the freezer for a couple hours if you want it more solid. If you don't want to eat it right away, store it in the freezer and allow it to thaw a bit before enjoying.

SOY-FREE   RAW   QUICK
TO PREPARE

CHOCOLATE PUDDING TARTS WITH AVOCADO

I used to love Jell-O chocolate pudding: I have magic memories of that sweet, rich creaminess. When I went vegan and started eating a more whole foods–focused diet, I realized I could create my own nourishing chocolate pudding that ticked all the boxes of what I loved about the Jell-O version, without the processed ingredients, dairy or plastic packaging. This recipe is it. The secret to the creaminess of the pudding is avocado! Just make sure to add enough sweetener and cacao; otherwise avocado chocolate pudding recipes can look a little green and not taste great. But when you do it right: oh, it's SO right.

SERVES 3 TO 6; MAKES 3 TARTS

CRUST
¾ cup (60 g) rolled oats

¾ cup (90 g) walnuts

1 cup (150 g) raisins

1 heaping tbsp (8 g) cacao powder

Pinch of sea salt

CHOCOLATE CREAM
½ cup (90 g) chopped avocado

¼ cup (60 ml) melted coconut oil

¼ cup (60 ml) brown rice syrup

2 pitted dates

2 tbsp (14 g) cacao powder

Pinch of sea salt

1 tbsp (15 ml) nondairy milk (page 209)

1 tsp vanilla extract

TOPPING
1 tbsp (10 g) sesame seeds

To make the crust, grind the oats and walnuts into a rough flour in a food processor. Add the raisins, cacao powder and salt and process until you have a crumbly yet sticky dough; it should hold its shape when pressed between two fingers. Press it into lined tart tins or any mold you like. Leave them in the fridge so they can set.

To make the chocolate cream, blend all the ingredients until smooth, thick and like whipped cream . . . but chocolate! Spread it into your tart crusts and leave it in the fridge for 1 to 2 hours, or overnight, so they can set.

Sprinkle with sesame seeds or anything else you like!

NUT-FREE **SOY-FREE** **RAW** **QUICK TO MAKE**

SPICED TAHINI DATE SHAKE

This is a rich shake that's gently flavored with chai spices; sweetened with dates, lucuma and stevia; and made creamy thanks to coconut milk, chia and frozen banana. It's a real comfort in cool and warm months, and it also has powerful reishi mushrooms snuck in, which are known to be rich in antioxidants and have anti-inflammatory, immunomodulating properties. Cloves are one of the most potent sources of antioxidants ever studied, according to its ORAC (Oxygen Radical Absorbance Capacity) score. I was inspired by two different recipes when I made this: one from Food52 and from Harmonic Arts.

SERVES 2; MAKES ~2½ CUPS (590 ML)

2 cups (480 ml) chilled Coconut Milk (page 209)

¼–⅛ tsp cardamom powder

¼ tsp ginger powder

½ tsp cinnamon powder

Pinch of stevia powder

2 cloves

1–2 tsp (2–5 g) reishi powder, as desired

2 pitted dates

1 frozen banana

1 tsp chia

1 tsp lucuma powder

4 ice cubes (optional)

Blend all the ingredients together until smooth and creamy. Adjust according to taste.

Add ice cubes if desired. You can blend them in or have the shake with whole ice cubes.

Pour into glasses and enjoy!

CHICKPEA COOKIE DOUGH

This one's filling and satisfying on its own or added to coconut ice cream, brownies, oatmeal, milkshakes and whatever else you like. Versatile chickpeas are full of fiber and protein, and eating legumes regularly may help to prevent heart disease, reduce the risk of developing type 2 diabetes and lower cholesterol. Feel free to adjust the amounts in this one to suit your own preferences (whether you want a more oaty cookie dough, a more gooey cookie dough, a more chocolaty cookie dough, etc.).

MAKES 3 CUPS (770 G)

2 cups (380 g) cooked chickpeas

½ cup (48 g) almond flour

½ cup (40 g) rolled oats

2 tbsp (14 g) ground flax seeds

Stevia

Pinch of sea salt

⅓ cup (60 g) almond butter

⅓ cup (80 ml) brown rice syrup, or more as desired

¼ cup (60 ml) almond milk

1 tsp vanilla extract

½ cup (90 g) roughly chopped Pure Chocolate (page 223)

Add the chickpeas, flour, oats, flax, stevia and salt to a food processor and process until the chickpeas have been broken down a bit.

Add the rest of the ingredients, except the chocolate, and process until you have a thick dough. Adjust according to taste, adding more brown rice syrup if you want it sweeter. Adjust according to consistency preference—if you'd like it thicker, add more nut butter; if you'd like it more crumbly, add more oats.

Transfer the dough to a bowl and mix in the chocolate chunks with a spoon.

Roll your cookie dough into balls or cookies, press into bars or leave in a giant hunk: it's up to you. Eat now if you want, but it's better after it sits in the fridge for a few hours or overnight.

Note: I like to coat mine in extra melted chocolate, like in the photo.

This will keep in the fridge for up to 2 weeks.

NUT-FREE   SOY-FREE   RAW

VANILLA COCONUT BUTTER CUPS WITH TAYBERRY JAM

Sooo peanut butter cups are rad and everything, but occasionally—only occasionally—I crave something other than chocolate and peanut butter. This is where coconut and berries come in. This recipe is light yet rich, and very coconut-y. Tayberries are new to me, I only found them at the farmers' market last summer and learned they are the engineered hybrid of blackberries and raspberries! SCIENCE!

**MAKES 6 LARGE CUPS,
OR 9 TO 12 MINI CUPS**

JAM

1 cup (150 g) tayberries

1 tbsp (15 ml) brown rice syrup

1 tbsp (15 ml) lime juice

2 tbsp (20 g) chia seeds, as needed

Pinch of stevia powder

½ tsp Elderflower Syrup (page 220) (optional)

VANILLA COCONUT BUTTER

1 cup (230 g) Coconut Butter (page 212)

¼ cup (60 ml) brown rice syrup

¼ cup (60 ml) melted coconut oil

Pinch of sea salt

1 tsp vanilla powder

Scant ¼ cup (60 ml) Coconut Milk (page 209), as needed

To make the jam, mash the berries into a paste, and then mix in the rest of the ingredients. Let it thicken up in the fridge for 20 to 30 minutes. If it's still too runny, add an extra tablespoon (10 g) of chia seeds.

To make the vanilla coconut butter, blend all the ingredients except the coconut milk together until smooth and very thick. It will be like a paste.

Using ¾ of this mixture (leave the rest in the blender, we'll use it in a minute), press it into the bottom and halfway up the sides of cupcake papers in a cupcake tin, or whatever molds you desire. You're basically forming a little bowl to spoon your jam into. Leave it in the freezer to harden up for 5 to 10 minutes.

Spoon the jam into your coconut butter cups and put it back in the fridge.

Add the coconut milk to the remaining vanilla coconut butter and blend until it's smooth and pourable. Pour evenly over your jam-filled coconut butter cups, sealing in the jam.

Sprinkle with salt, slivered almonds, chia seeds or whatever else you want. Leave in the freezer or fridge until they've hardened up (around 30 to 60 minutes), and enjoy!

CHEWY GINGER COOKIES

These bring me back to the winter holidays of my youth. Thanks to the fresh ginger in here, the cookies are a little spicy. Molasses provides iron, calcium and that strong, unique flavor that defines gingersnaps. Cinnamon and ginger are terrific for blood health and fighting inflammation, and oats provide fiber and a bit of protein. The maple syrup lends a wonderful flavor but, for me anyways, its sweetness isn't needed here (the dates, raisins and molasses are sweet enough).

MAKES ~12 MEDIUM COOKIES; 24 SMALL

2 cups (160 g) rolled oats

1 cup (170 g) pitted dates

½ cup (75 g) raisins

2 tbsp (30 g) of grated ginger

1 tbsp (15 ml) blackstrap molasses

1 tbsp (15 ml) brown rice syrup

2 tbsp (28 g) melted coconut oil

1 tsp lemon juice

½ tsp cinnamon powder

⅛ tsp salt

1 tsp vanilla extract

Ground flax seed, as needed

Raw sugar (optional)

Cinnamon powder (optional)

Grind the oats into flour in a food processor.

Next, blend all the ingredients together, including the flour, in your food processor until it forms into a ball of slightly sticky, slightly crumbly dough. It should hold its shape when pressed between two fingers. If it's too crumbly, add more coconut oil or a tablespoon (15 ml) of water. If it's too moist, add 1 tablespoon (7 g) of ground flax seed.

On parchment paper, shape it into as many balls as you desire and then stamp them down with the bottom of a glass or jar. Sprinkle them with some raw sugar, or cinnamon powder, and leave in the fridge for 3 to 5 hours, or overnight, so they can harden.*

*Alternatively, place the ball of dough in between two sheets of parchment paper, and roll it out thinly until it's the thickness you want for your cookies. Leave in the fridge for an hour, then use a cookie cutter to cut out cookies from the flattened dough. Once the cookies are cut, put them back in the fridge for another 2 hours, or overnight, until they are solid.

SOY-FREE

RAW

QUICK TO PREPARE

MOCHA MOUSSE WITH CARDAMOM + COCONUT

This is my take on chocolate mousse—vamped up with coffee, coconut, hazelnuts, cardamom and berries. It's not too sweet and is high in fiber, selenium, antioxidants, calcium, manganese, magnesium and phosphorus thanks to Brazil nuts, chia seeds and cacao. It's luscious as heck and delicious for breakfast or dessert.

SERVES 4 TO 5; MAKES ~2½ CUPS (610 G)

MOUSSE

2½ cups (590 ml) canned coconut milk

3 tbsp (17 g) decaffeinated ground coffee beans

3 tbsp (21 g) cacao powder

3 tbsp (45 ml) melted coconut oil

4 tbsp (40 g) chia seeds

⅛ tsp stevia powder

⅛ tsp cardamom powder

⅓ cup (56 g) hazelnuts

¼ cup (38 g) Brazil nuts

1 tsp vanilla extract

Pinch of sea salt

¼ cup (60 ml) brown rice syrup or maple syrup, as desired

TO SERVE

¾ cup (175 ml) Whipped Coconut Cream (page 206)

4 tbsp (25 g) shaved dark chocolate

2 tbsp (13 g) coffee beans

¼ cup (38 g) raspberries (or other berries)

Blend all the mousse ingredients until smooth. Adjust according to taste, adding syrup as desired. It should be the consistency of yogurt at this time.

Pour it into ramekins, jars or cups and leave in the fridge overnight so they can thicken up.

Serve with the whipped coconut cream, chocolate, coffee beans and berries. Best enjoyed within 2 days.

SWEET POTATO BROWNIES WITH DATE CARAMEL FROSTING

This is adapted from one of my fave recipes I've ever published on my blog. It's rich in cacao flavor, and not overly sweet. It's delicious with any frosting you like, but I love a salted caramel situation. Sweet potatoes are high in beta-carotene (vitamin A), vitamin C, potassium and fiber.

SERVES 16; MAKES 16 BROWNIES

BROWNIES

1 small to medium cooked sweet potato, roughly chopped

1½ cups (260 g) cooked black beans

⅓ cup (57 g) pitted Medjool dates

½ cup (55 g) cacao powder

¾ cup (72 g) almond flour

1 tbsp (7 g) ground flax seed

1 tbsp (11 g) baking powder

¼ cup (55 g) coconut oil

½ cup (120 ml) nondairy milk (page 209)

1 tsp vanilla extract

½ tsp sea salt

1–2 tbsp (5–12 g) ground coffee beans (optional)

FROSTING

½ cup (85 g) dates, or more as needed

½ cup (120 ml) Almond Milk (page 210)

1 tsp lemon juice

¼ tsp sea salt

1 heaping tbsp (11 g) almond butter

1 tbsp (14 g) cacao butter wafers, or coconut oil, melted

1 heaping tbsp (8 g) cacao powder (optional, if you want chocolate frosting)

Preheat the oven to 350°F (177°C).

To make the brownies, throw everything into a food processor or blender and process until you have a thick, wet batter. If you want the brownies to be a bit firmer once baked, add a cup (96 g) more of flour at this point.

Pour the batter into a lined pan and bake for 30 to 40 minutes or until they smell ready and a fork or toothpick comes out clean. If you'd like them less fudgy, bake for the entire 40 minutes. Let them cool for 30 to 60 minutes.

To make the frosting, let the dates sit in the almond milk for 10 minutes, and then blend together all the ingredients until smooth.

Frost your brownies, slice and enjoy! These will keep for a week in the fridge.

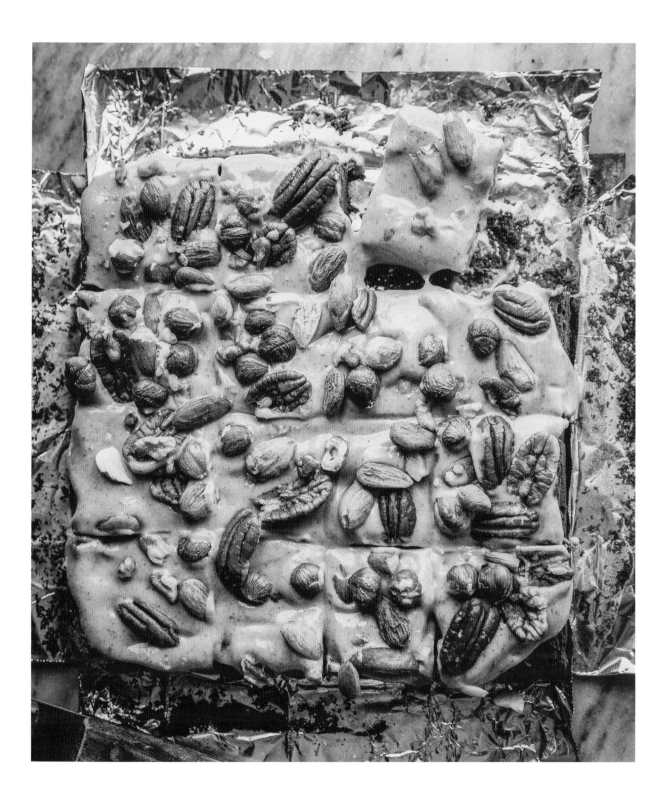

NUT-FREE

SOY-FREE

RAW

QUICK
TO MAKE

AVOCADO SHAKE WITH SALTED CHOCOLATE SAUCE

My parents lived in Indonesia for a number of years before they started a family in "Canada" (AKA Turtle Island). Their memories of avocado shakes with chocolate sauce (*jus alpukat*) immediately intrigued me. I researched traditional recipes—which often use condensed cow's milk and sugar—and developed my own version with coconut milk and brown rice syrup. I must say: this drink is divine. It's unbelievably creamy and just sweet enough. If you haven't experienced *jus alpukat* yet, you are in for a treat. Avocados are full of healthy, monounsaturated fatty acids, fiber and nutrients such as vitamin K, potassium, folate and vitamin C. They contain anti-cancer properties and may help lower cholesterol and triglyceride levels.

SERVES 2 TO 3; MAKES ~3 CUPS (710 ML)

SALTED CHOCOLATE SAUCE

1 tbsp (15 ml) melted coconut oil

1 tbsp (7 g) cacao powder

⅛ tsp sea salt, or smoked salt, to taste

1 tsp brown rice syrup

2 tbsp (30 ml) warm water, as needed

SHAKE

3 avocados

1 cup (240 ml) Coconut Milk (page 209)

½ cup (70 g) ice cubes

⅛ tsp stevia powder

2 tbsp (30 ml) brown rice syrup

Pinch of sea salt

To make the sauce, whisk or stir together the ingredients until smooth, adding as much salt as you prefer. If it's too thick, add a bit of water.

To make the shake, blend all the ingredients until smooth, adding ice as desired to get the consistency you want.

Drizzle the sauce into glasses, pour in your shake and drizzle more chocolate on top. Enjoy with straws!

SOY-FREE   RAW   QUICK
TO MAKE

CACAO BUTTER BARK WITH LUCUMA, VANILLA + CORDYCEPS

Cacao butter is a divine food, in my humble opinion: its smell, texture, richness … oh, honey *swoon*! Lucuma and baobab add natural, low-glycemic sweetness; tahini provides iron; and cordyceps, ashwagandha and *maca* offer adaptogenic power.

SERVES ~18; MAKES 3 CHOCOLATE BARS

BARK
½ cup (80 g) cacao butter wafers

¼ cup (60 g) tahini, or cashew butter

¼ cup (60 ml) maple syrup, as desired

2 tbsp (14 g) lucuma powder

2 tbsp (14 g) cordyceps powder

1 tbsp (7 g) maca powder

1 tsp baobab powder

1 tsp ashwagandha powder

½ tsp vanilla powder

½ tsp vanilla extract

Pinch of stevia powder

Pinch of sea salt

CRUNCHY BITS
¼ cup (43 g) almonds

¼ cup (38 g) Brazil nuts

TOPPINGS
3 tbsp (30 g) hemp seeds

3 tbsp (14 g) shredded coconut

To make the bark, melt the cacao butter wafers in a heavy-bottomed pot on low, and then turn off the heat.

Whisk in the rest of the ingredients until smooth, adding as much sweetener as you like. It will be a little thin at this point, like the consistency of cream.

Roughly chop the crunchy bits and stir them into your cacao mixture.

Pour the mixture into a lined pan and sprinkle with the toppings.

Leave it in the freezer for 20 minutes, or until it has solidified. Keep in the fridge for 2 or 3 weeks, or in the freezer for a month.

SOY-FREE

RAW

QUICK
TO MAKE

ADAPTOGENIC WHITE CHOCOLATE

This is a creamy, rich, fragrant recipe full of cacao butter flavor. It has mood-boosting properties thanks to mucuna, astragalus and ashwagandha. Wonderful combined with almond butter and dates.

**SERVES 18; MAKES
3 CHOCOLATE BARS**

1 cup (160 g) cacao butter wafers

⅓ cup (73 g) Coconut Butter
(page 212)

1½ tsp (4 g) mucuna pruriens
powder

¼ cup (20 g) tocotrienols

½ tsp vanilla powder

½ tsp vanilla extract

1 tbsp (7 g) astragalus powder

1 tbsp (7 g) ashwagandha powder

Pinch of sea salt

Pinch of stevia powder

½ cup (55 g) cashews, or ¼ cup
(44 g) cashew butter

⅓ cup (80 ml) maple syrup, as
desired

OPTIONAL TOPPING
½ cup (75 g) berries

Melt the cacao and coconut butter in a heavy-bottomed pan on low, and then turn off the heat.

Whisk in the rest of the ingredients, except the cashews, until smooth. Add maple syrup as desired.

Transfer everything, including the cashews, to a blender and blend until smooth and thick.

Pour or spread the mixture into chocolate molds, or onto a lined plate or pan, and sprinkle with berries (if using). I'd recommend gently squishing the berries with your fingers as you sprinkle them on.

Leave this in the freezer for 20 minutes or until it has solidified. Store in the freezer for up to a month.

BANANA COCONUT MILKSHAKE WITH GINGER CARAMEL

Heaven. Ever since I tried the milkshake recipe from Virpi Mikkonen and Tuulia Talvio's cookbook, *N'ice Cream*, I have been in love with their method. Basically the milkshake is super rich and not making any apologies for itself. (Personal goals, if I'm being honest.)

SERVES 2 TO 3

SHAKE
1 (13.5-oz [400-ml]) can full-fat coconut milk, left in the fridge overnight

3 chopped, frozen bananas

1 tsp vanilla extract

1–2 tbsp (15–30 ml) brown rice syrup, as desired

GINGER CARAMEL
2 tbsp (22 g) almond butter

1 tbsp (15 ml) maple syrup

2 tbsp (30 ml) Coconut Milk (page 209)

¼ tsp ginger powder, or more as desired

To make the shake, scoop out the thick coconut fat that should have set in the top of the can. This is ideally what you want to use, or else use the entire can. Blend all the ingredients together until smooth.

To make the caramel, whisk all the ingredients together until smooth, adding ginger as desired.

Pour a little caramel into glasses, scoop in some milkshake and keep doing this until you've used up all the caramel and milkshake.

This one's best enjoyed immediately, with Dark Chocolate Almond Butter Fudge chunks (page 131).

Alternatively, scoop the shake into a jar and put in the freezer for ice cream later! Just don't fill up the jar entirely, or else the glass will break! Before enjoying, let it thaw for a few minutes (unless you're one of those who prefers really hard ice cream).

SOY-FREE   RAW   QUICK
TO PREPARE

LEMON GINGER VANILLA CREAM TARTS

The lusciousness of this recipe takes me to another world. I love the tartness of the lemon paired with spicy ginger and sweet coconut cream. Perfect in summer. Note: the crust on these is so good that I'd recommend doubling the recipe, shaping the extra dough into balls, bars or cookies and keeping them in the fridge for easy-to-grab sweet, nutty bites.

SERVES 6 TO 12; MAKES 6 TARTS

CRUST
1 cup (80 g) rolled oats

1 cup (110 g) cashews

2 tbsp (30 ml) maple syrup

2 tbsp (28 g) coconut oil

½ cup (80 g) sesame seeds

LEMON CREAM
1 (13.5-oz [400-ml]) can full-fat coconut milk

½ cup (120 ml) lemon juice

½ tsp vanilla powder

⅓ cup (80 ml) Ginger Syrup (page 219), or brown rice syrup + 1 tsp chunk peeled ginger

⅙ cup (40 g) coconut oil

Pinch of sea salt

Scant tsp stevia powder

3 tbsp (30 g) chia seeds

To make the crust, grind the oats and cashews into flour in a blender or food processor.

Transfer to a bowl and mix in the rest of the ingredients. You want a thick dough that will hold its shape when pressed between two fingers. If it's too crumbly, add a tablespoon (15 ml) of water, or extra coconut oil or maple syrup.

Press it into lined tart tins and leave in the fridge for 20 to 30 minutes until they harden up.

To make the cream, scoop off the thick, solid fat in the can of coconut milk; this is what you want to use. Add it to a blender, and blend all the ingredients together, except the chia seeds, until smooth. Stir in the chia seeds. Leave this mixture in the fridge for 2 hours so it can thicken; then scoop it into your tart crusts. Leave them in the fridge overnight so they can set.

EARL GREY CHOCOLATE ICE CREAM

This recipe is deeply delicious, but it has a secret ingredient that most people would probably never want near their ice cream: beans. (Navy beans, to be exact.) Sounds gross, but they actually add a creamy texture, a bunch of nutrition, and very mild flavor that works well with the cacao and earl grey. The inspiration for using navy beans in ice cream comes from an experience I had in Ottawa—the traditional, unceded territory of the Algonquin Anishinaabeg people—at a small-batch ice-cream shop called Moo Shu, where they used it in a vegan Earl Grey flavor.

SERVES 8; MAKES ~4 CUPS (610 G)

1½ cups (355 ml) full-fat coconut milk

1½ cups (255 g) cooked navy beans

1 cup (170 g) pitted dates, or agave syrup

⅓ cup (80 ml) strong-brewed earl grey tea, chilled or room temperature

2 tbsp (14 g) cacao powder

1 tsp vanilla extract

⅛ tsp sea salt

⅛ tsp stevia powder

Blend all the ingredients together until very smooth. Adjust according to taste, adding more sweetener or cacao if desired.

If you have an ice-cream maker, use it now. Or go with the simplest method and just pour into freezer-friendly containers before freezing.

Otherwise, pour the ice-cream batter into ice-cube trays and allow it to solidify in the freezer.

Remove from the ice-cube trays and blend in a blender or food processor until smooth. This will take a few minutes, and you will probably have to stop and scrape down the sides of the food processor to keep getting everything evenly blended.

Eat it now as soft serve, and/or keep it in the freezer in jars or freezer-friendly containers. Don't fill the jars up all the way though, because they will crack! The ice cream will keep for up to 3 months but is best within 1 month.

Before enjoying, let it thaw for a few minutes (unless you're one of those who prefers really hard ice cream).

SOY-FREE   QUICK
            TO MAKE

COOKIE DOUGH ICE CREAM SHAKE

This shake's extra decadent topped with liquid Pure Chocolate (page 223). The coconut milk adds a wonderful richness here, and I am a big fan of cookie-dough-anything. This is a dairy-free delight that sneakily provides fiber, protein, potassium, iron and healthy fats. It's not overwhelmingly sweet, so I can enjoy more of it without feeling that sugar burn in my mouth. If you want it sweeter, however, I'd recommend adding date chunks or extra syrup.

SERVES 2 TO 3

1 (13.5-oz [400-ml]) can full-fat coconut milk, left in the fridge overnight

2 frozen bananas

½ tsp vanilla extract

Pinch of sea salt

2 tbsp (30 ml) brown rice syrup

3 dates, pitted and torn apart, as desired

½ batch Chickpea Cookie Dough (page 176)

To make the shake, scoop out the thick, white coconut cream that should have set in the top of the can: this is what you want to use (if this doesn't happen, don't worry about it—your shake just won't be as thick).

Blend all the ingredients together—except the cookie dough—until smooth and delicious. Add sweetener if desired.

Form the cookie dough into bite-size balls or chunks. Pour the shake into glasses or bowls, adding cookie dough balls as you go. Add date pieces if you want. Top with more cookie dough chunks. Enjoy immediately!

NUT-FREE   SOY-FREE   RAW   QUICK TO MAKE

COCONUT VANILLA FLOATS

If you'd like this all raw, use Banana Ice Cream (page 216) or a homemade raw ice cream. If you are looking for a more root beer-y flavor, you could use root beer extract. Coconut water is not for everyone, so taste test to decide if you like it on its own first. If it's not your thing, you could add some nice ginger kombucha instead (which tastes like ginger ale, in my opinion). Coconut water is hydrating and replenishing thanks to its electrolyte content (in fact it contains more potassium than most sports drinks), so I like to drink it after I've been sweating or exercising.

SERVES 2

2 cups (480 ml) chilled coconut water

¼ cup (43 g) pitted dates

1 tsp vanilla extract

½ tsp lemon juice (optional)

Pinch of sea salt

⅔ cups (90 g) your fave vegan ice cream

Blend all the ingredients, except the ice cream, until smooth.

Pour into glasses and scoop in your ice cream. Enjoy immediately.

SOY-FREE   **RAW**

CHEWY CHOCOLATE CARAMEL CANDY BARS

Fudgy, coconut-y, caramel-y dreams become reality. This is one of the most decadent recipes in here and it will not disappoint if you are craving a sweet chocolate treat. Behind-the-scenes, it also happens to provide a bunch of fiber and healthy fats thanks to the oats and nuts; and some iron and zinc from the cacao.

MAKES 12 BARS

BASE
1 cup (80 g) rolled oats
½ cup (56 g) coconut flour
1–2 tbsp (15–30 ml) melted coconut oil, as needed
2 tbsp (30 ml) brown rice syrup
1 tsp lemon juice

COCONUT FILLING
1 cup (218 g) Coconut Butter (page 212)
½ cup (55 g) cashews
¼ cup (60 ml) brown rice syrup
¼ cup (60 ml) coconut milk, as needed
1 tsp vanilla extract

CARAMEL
¾ cup (128 g) pitted dates
¼ cup (62 g) almond butter
¼ cup (60 ml) water, or more as needed
2 tbsp (30 ml) melted coconut oil
1 tsp lemon juice
½ tsp vanilla powder
Pinch of sea salt

CHOCOLATE FUDGE
⅔ cup (73 g) cacao powder
⅔ cup (180 ml) brown rice syrup
½ cup (120 ml) melted coconut oil
2–3 tbsp (30–45 ml) coconut milk, as needed

To make the base, grind the oats into flour in a food processor. Add the remaining ingredients and process until you have a crumbly cookie dough. It should hold its shape when pressed between your fingers. Press into the bottom of a lined pan and leave in the freezer.

To make the coconut filling, blend all the ingredients together until smooth. Add coconut milk as needed to get a thick, creamy consistency. If it's still too thick to blend, add more coconut milk as needed. Spread evenly over your cookie base and put it back in the freezer.

To make the caramel, blend all the ingredients together until smooth. Spread evenly over your coconut filling and put back in the freezer. Leave it there for at least a few hours, or overnight, or until it sets. Slice into bars with a sharp knife.

To make the chocolate fudge, whisk together the ingredients until smooth. If it gets too solid, remelt over low heat. You need it to be a consistency you can drizzle, so whisk in coconut milk as needed.

Drizzle the chocolate over your bars—or coat them completely—and leave them in the fridge or freezer so the chocolate can harden; it will take around 20 minutes. These will keep in the fridge for up to 2 weeks, or in the freezer for up to 2 months.

BASIC RECIPES, SAUCES & SYRUPS

This chapter provides recipes for nondairy staples like yogurt, milk and cheese; basic formulas for chocolate, crackers and syrups; quick, powdered drink mixes; as well as a bunch of my favorite sauces, dressings and spreads. Most of these are called for as parts of other recipes in this cookbook, but of course feel free to use them in your own innovative forms.

NUT-FREE   SOY-FREE   QUICK
                       TO MAKE

WHIPPED COCONUT CREAM

I am coconut's #1 fan, so I am all about whipped coco cream. It's very easy and quick to make, given that you have a good can of coconut milk to start with. Light coconut milk will not do; full-fat coconut milk works well. Try to find a brand with as few preservatives as possible, you want coconut and water to be the only ingredients. If the coconut milk has preservatives in it that inhibit separation, it may not be able to be turned into whipped cream. Ashlae, creator of one of my fave recipe blogs, Oh Lady Cakes, recommends Savoy and Aroy-D brands for the best whipped cream. This recipe is used in my recipes for Mocha Mousse (page 183), Pumpkin Patch Smoothies (page 39), Pumpkin Pie (page 161), Chocolate Pudding Tarts (page 172) and Lemon Ginger Vanilla Cream Tarts (page 195).

MAKES ~1 CUP (240 ML), DEPENDING ON THE FAT CONTENT IN YOUR CAN OF COCONUT MILK

1 (13.5-oz [400-ml]) can full-fat or premium canned coconut milk

OPTIONAL
½ tsp vanilla extract
Pinch of stevia powder

Let the can of coconut milk sit in your fridge for 24 hours so the coconut cream can separate from the water.

Open the can from the bottom and pour out the water (or use it in smoothies), revealing the thick, white, fatty goodness underneath.

Scoop this out and whisk into whipped cream, by hand or in a mixer (it should take 1 to 2 minutes). I've used a food processor and blender before, but it will only take a sec, so watch closely!

Add the vanilla and stevia if you like.

MILKS

Nondairy milks are easy and quick to make (once your nuts or grains have soaked), in small or big batches. You can use whatever nuts, seeds, fruits or pseudo-grains you want, and the ratios are generally going to be the same. Here I provide some example recipes so you get an idea of how to make your own. I like to add a pinch of salt to enhance the flavors, and please feel free to add sweetener and spices like vanilla, and cinnamon. I have left the recipes mostly plain here, so you can customize as desired.

Note: Don't throw out the leftover nut pulp! I provide a few recipes you can use it in on page 120 and page 231. Or else, keep it in bags in the freezer and add it to baked goods at your own discretion.

NUT-FREE   SOY-FREE   RAW   QUICK TO MAKE

HEMP MILK

MAKES ~1 LITER (34 OZ)

1 cup (160 g) hemp seeds
3–4 cups (710–950 ml) water
Pinch of sea salt

Blend all the ingredients until smooth. If you want a thicker, richer milk, use 3 cups (710 ml) of water. If you want a lighter milk, use 4 cups (950 ml) of water.

Strain it through a nut milk bag or cheesecloth.

Pour it into airtight containers and store it in the fridge for up to a week. Shake before using!

NUT-FREE   SOY-FREE   QUICK TO MAKE

COCONUT MILK

MAKES ~1 LITER (34 OZ)

2 cups (480 ml) canned coconut milk (or 1 cup [75 g] coconut flakes)
3–4 cups (710–950 ml) water
Pinch of sea salt

Blend all the ingredients until smooth. If you want a thicker, richer milk, use 3 cups (710 ml) of water. If you want a lighter milk, use 4 cups (950 ml) of water.

If you used coconut flakes, strain it through a nut milk bag or cheesecloth.

Pour into airtight containers and store in the fridge for up to a week. Shake before using!

ALMOND-BRAZIL NUT MILK

SOY-FREE **RAW** **QUICK TO MAKE**

MAKES ~1 LITER (34 OZ)

½ cup (85 g) almonds, soaked for 8–12 hours

½ cup (76 g) Brazil nuts, soaked for 2–3 hours

3–4 cups (710–950) water

Pinch of sea salt

Blend all the ingredients until smooth. If you want a thicker, richer milk, use 3 cups (710 ml) of water. If you want a lighter milk, use 4 cups (950 ml) of water.

Strain it through a nut milk bag or cheesecloth.

Pour it into airtight containers and store in the fridge for up to a week. Shake before using!

OAT MILK

NUT-FREE **SOY-FREE** **RAW** **QUICK TO MAKE**

MAKES ~1 LITER (34 OZ)

1 cup (80 g) rolled oats, soaked for 12 hours

3–4 cups (710–950) water

Pinch of sea salt

Blend all the ingredients until smooth. If you want a thicker, richer milk, use 3 cups (710 ml) of water. If you want a lighter milk, use 4 cups (950 ml) of water.

Strain it through a nut milk bag or cheesecloth.

Pour into airtight containers and store in the fridge for up to a week. Shake before using!

RICE MILK

NUT-FREE **SOY-FREE** **RAW** **QUICK TO MAKE**

MAKES ~1 LITER (34 OZ)

1 cup (210 g) white or brown rice, soaked for 24–48 hours, or cooked

3–4 cups (710–950 ml) water

Pinch of sea salt

Blend all the ingredients until smooth. If you want a thicker, richer milk, use 3 cups (710 ml) of water. If you want a lighter milk, use 4 cups (950 ml) of water.

Strain through a nut milk bag or cheesecloth.

Pour into airtight containers and store in the fridge for up to a week. Shake before using!

CHOCOLATE MILK

SOY-FREE

RAW

**QUICK
TO MAKE**

MAKES ~2 CUPS (480 ML)

2 cups (480 ml) fave nondairy
milk (page 209)

1 tbsp (7 g) cacao powder

1 tbsp (7 g) mesquite powder

1 tbsp (11 g) almond butter

2–3 pitted dates

Blend all the ingredients until smooth.

Enjoy fresh!

STRAWBERRY MILK

SOY-FREE

RAW

**QUICK
TO MAKE**

MAKES ~2 CUPS (480 ML)

2 cups (480 ml) fave nondairy
milk (page 209)

1 cup (150 g) strawberries

Pinch of stevia powder

½ tsp vanilla powder

Blend all the ingredients until smooth.

Enjoy fresh!

COCONUT BUTTER

This is one of my favorite foods. I eat it on its own every day and add it to smoothies, cookies and oatmeal regularly for that creamy, coconut essence. I highly recommend using the Twister Jar attachment with a Blendtec blender here. (A strong food processor or a high-speed blender will work, but it takes a bit more time and labor. The Twister Jar makes this recipe effortless and ready in literally a minute.) Note: coconut flour will not work for this! There is too little fat, and adding coconut oil back into coconut flour is a no-go as well. Trust me: I have tried. This recipe is used in my Turmeric + Black Pepper Elixir (page 23), Protein-Packed Vanilla Banana Shake (page 44), Vanilla Coconut Butter Cups with Tayberry Jam (page 179), Adaptogenic White Chocolate (page 191) and Chewy Chocolate Caramel Candy Bars (page 203).

MAKES JUST UNDER 2 CUPS (440 G)

3 cups (230 g) shredded coconut, or coconut flakes

OPTIONAL ADD-INS
½ tsp vanilla powder

Pinch of stevia, or 1 tsp maple syrup

In a high-speed blender, grind the shredded coconut until it becomes a thick paste (aka coconut butter!). You may have to stop blending a few times to let the machine cool down and/or push the coconut towards the blades so it is all evenly ground up.

Keep it in jars in the fridge for up to a month, where it will harden up; or at room temperature in a cool, dark place for up to 2 weeks, where it stays softer.

NUT-FREE

SOY-FREE

RAW

QUICK
TO MAKE

EASY COCONUT YOGURT

It may take you a few tries to get the knack for yogurt-making, but when you do, it's a rewarding moment. This recipe is the easiest, most streamlined method I have found, and it only asks for two ingredients: coconut milk and probiotic capsules. If your probiotic is strong (like 50 billion active cultures), you don't need as many. If your probiotic is lighter (like 15 to 25 billion), use a couple more. If you want a thicker yogurt, add a teaspoon of ground chia seeds once it's fermented. This recipe is used in the Coco Yogurt Bowl on page 135. I additionally recommend pairing the yogurt with my granola recipe on page 156. Fermented foods are great for gut health, which is essential for overall physical well-being!

**MAKES JUST UNDER
2 CUPS (470 ML)**

YOGURT
1 (13.5-oz [400-ml]) can full-fat coconut milk

3–5 probiotic capsules

ADD-INS
1 tsp vanilla extract, or powder

Pinch stevia powder

2 tbsp (30 ml) maple syrup

1 tbsp (10 g) chia seeds

Pour the coconut milk into a clean glass jar.

Open the capsules and mix the probiotics evenly into the coconut milk. Cover the top of the jar with a cloth and rubber band, or place a lid on top, but do not screw it on all the way.

Leave in a warm spot for 24 to 48 hours (examples: wrapped in a towel, in the oven with the oven light on, in a yogurt maker, etc.) or until you see a few bubbles and it begins to smell and taste like, well, yogurt. Check on it periodically.

Keep it in the fridge for up to 3 weeks.

BANANA ICE CREAM

A summer fave, and game-changer for ice cream lovers who enjoy (or at least don't mind) banana flavor, I'm keeping this recipe basic here, but my favorite way to make this is blending in cocoa powder and some dates.

SERVES 1 TO 3

ICE CREAM
2–3 frozen bananas

OPTIONAL ADD-INS
½ tsp vanilla powder

1 tbsp (15 ml) brown rice syrup

Splash of nondairy milk
(page 209)

Other flavorings like chocolate, matcha, berries, etc.

2–3 dates

Blend the bananas until smooth. A high-speed blender really makes a difference, but a food processor will work too. It may take a few minutes to get it totally smooth, and you may have to stop the appliance a couple times to scrape down the sides. Be patient; it will suddenly turn into a wonderful soft serve consistency. When this happens, stop.

Eat right away!

GINGER SYRUP

Sooo yes, this recipe does include sugar as an ingredient. Don't flip out. I believe eating "healthfully" means more than only eating the most nutritionally-dense foods possible at every meal. There's much more to health than just diet. If you really don't wanna use plain ole sugar in this recipe, you can use maple syrup and a bit of water, instead of the sugar and water. This syrup is wonderful in tea. Use more ginger if you want it spicier! This recipe is used in Dandelion Chocolate Lattes (page 56), Matcha Ginger Ice Cream (page 171), and Lemon Ginger Vanilla Cream Tarts (page 195).

MAKES ¾ CUP (180 ML)

1 cup (190 g) sugar

1 cup (240 ml) water

⅓–½ cup (75–115 g) grated ginger, as desired

Combine the sugar and water in a pot on medium-high heat, stirring until the sugar dissolves.

Add the ginger and bring it to a boil. Boil for 10 minutes, stirring often.

Reduce the temperature to medium-low and simmer for another 8 to 10 minutes.

Strain the syrup into a bottle or jar, let cool and store in the pantry or fridge for up to 3 months.

Psst: don't throw out the strained ginger! It's yummy to eat as is, or added to smoothies, oatmeal or baked goods.

ELDERFLOWER SYRUP

Here's a delightfully floral addition to summery drinks or herbal teas. If you don't wanna use plain sugar in this recipe, you can use maple syrup instead of the sugar and water, and infuse the maple syrup with the elderflowers for 2 to 4 weeks, covered in a bowl or jar, in a cool, dark place. This recipe is used on page 27, in a spiced drink, and in Vanilla Coconut Butter Cups with Tayberry Jam (page 179).

MAKES ~1½ CUPS (355 ML)

1 cup (190 g) sugar
1 cup (240 ml) water
1 cup (33 g) elderflowers

Combine the sugar and water in a pot on medium-high heat, stirring until the sugar dissolves.

Add the elderflowers to the pot and bring to a boil. Boil for 10 minutes.

Reduce the temperature to medium-low and simmer until the syrup has thickened and is fragrant, around 15 to 20 minutes.

Strain the syrup into a bottle, let cool and store in the pantry or fridge for up to 3 months.

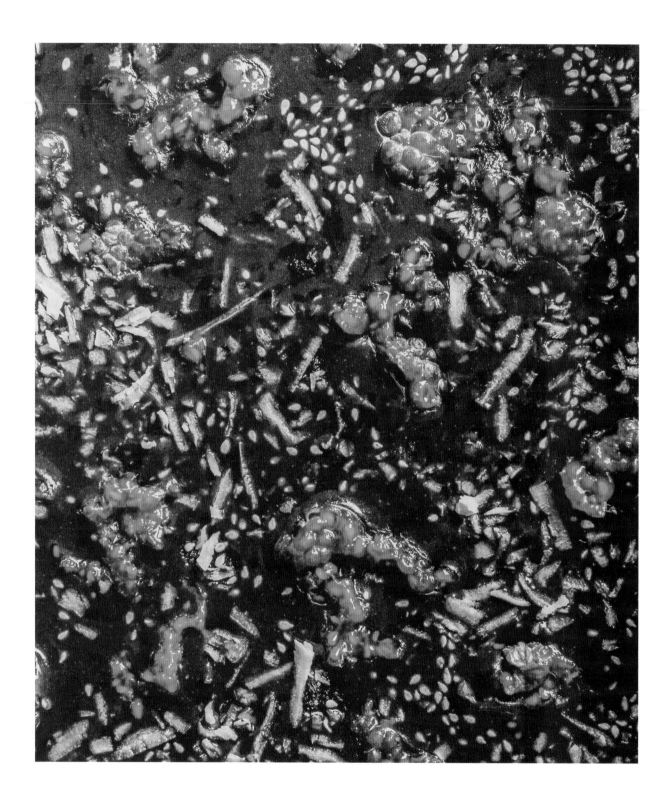

NUT-FREE   SOY-FREE   RAW   QUICK TO MAKE

PURE CHOCOLATE

I have kept this as simple as possible so it can be used as a base for any other recipes you like. Add whatever your heart desires and use this recipe in any others you wish. It is, of course, enchanting all on its own. If you want chewier chocolate, use brown rice syrup instead of maple.

MAKES 3 CHOCOLATE BARS; 1½ CUPS (200 G)

¾ cup (173 g) cacao butter, or coconut oil

⅔ cup + 1 tbsp (65 g) cacao powder

2–3 tbsp (30–45 ml) maple syrup, as desired

ADD-INS
Pinch of sea salt

1 tsp vanilla extract

¼ cup (19 g) shredded coconut

¼ cup (38 g) mushy raspberries

1 tbsp (10 g) sesame seeds

Melt the cacao butter or coconut oil in a heavy-bottomed pot on low heat. Once melted, turn off the heat (it'll take a few minutes).

Whisk in the rest of the ingredients, adding more maple syrup according to your taste preferences, and adding salt and vanilla if desired. The mixture should become smooth, but be easily poured.

Pour into chocolate molds (or onto a lined plate or pan), add extra toppings if you want, and leave in the fridge or freezer for 20 minutes, or until hardened.

Store in the fridge for up to 3 months. You can remelt the chocolate for chocolate sauce in other recipes.

NUT-FREE   **SOY-FREE**   **RAW**   **QUICK TO MAKE**

ROSEMARY LEMON WATER

This recipe is ridiculously simple and wonderful to sip any time of day and year. Rosemary is often used in aromatherapy and can help improve your mood and calm your mind. Lemon aids digestion, is rich in vitamin C and frankly just makes water taste better.

SERVES 1 TO 2

4 cups (1 L) boiled water

2 tbsp (5 g) fresh rosemary leaves

2 tbsp (30 ml) lemon juice

In a jar or mug, pour the water over the rosemary and let it steep for 10 to 15 minutes. Add the lemon juice and enjoy right away, or let it cool and have with ice later.

SOY-FREE   RAW   QUICK
                   TO PREPARE

CASHEW CHEESE WITH GARLIC + HERBES DE PROVENCE

The miso adds rich, sweet and rounded umami flavor to this creamy cheese. I love spreading this on toast with avocado slices and some Garlic Buttery Spread (page 244); or serving with Seedy Herby Crackers (page 231). This recipe is used in Garden Lasagna (page 103) and Shiitake Mushroom Pasta (page 104).

MAKES ~3 CUPS (360 G)

2 cups (220 g) cashews, soaked for 2 hours

½ cup (120 ml) lemon juice

1 tsp garlic powder

2–3 tbsp (30–45 ml) water, if needed

1 tbsp (2 g) herbes de provence

1 tsp (5 g) miso paste (optional)

Salt and pepper, as desired

Blend all the ingredients together until smooth; it should be very thick. Add water if it's too thick for your blender or food processor to handle.

Adjust according to taste, adding salt as desired.

Form the cheese into a log or wheel and coat in extra herbes de provence, salt and pepper; or simply scoop it into a container if you don't mind the form.

Wrap the cheese in parchment paper, or cover if it's in a container. Let the cheese sit at room temperature for 2 to 5 days or until it has firmed up and developed sharper notes. Or if you like it as is, put it in the fridge now. Keep in the fridge for up to 3 weeks; it will develop more flavor as time passes.

SOY-FREE RAW OPTION QUICK TO MAKE

PAPRIKA GARLIC CRACKERS

These are smoky, cheesy and savory. I eat a lot of the raw dough before it gets in the oven. Once baked, their crunch is satisfying and pairs perfectly with fresh salads, creamy soups and dips like Hummus (page 254). They're also delicious crumbled and added on top of pasta dishes. This recipe is used in the Big Ole Salad (page 91).

MAKES ~35 BITE-SIZE CRACKERS

¾ cup (72 g) almond flour

¾ cup (69 g) chickpea flour

¾ cup (112 g) sesame seeds

⅓–½ cup (54–80 g) hemp seeds

¼ cup (28 g) ground flax seed

¼ cup (20 g) nutritional yeast

1 tbsp (8 g) garlic powder

½ tsp smoked paprika powder

Salt and pepper, as desired

¼ cup (60 ml) extra-virgin olive oil

¼ cup (60 ml) lemon juice

¼ cup (60 ml) water

Preheat the oven to 350°F (177°C).

Stir together the dry ingredients evenly. Then add the wet ingredients and mix everything together until you have a thick, moist dough. Adjust according to taste.

Spread the dough onto a sheet of parchment paper on a baking sheet, with a second piece of parchment on top. Roll out evenly with a rolling pin until the dough is about an inch (2.5-cm) thick. Take off the top piece of parchment.

Score with a knife or pizza cutter into whatever sizes and shapes you desire; just make sure they're all relatively similar.

Bake for 15 minutes, or until the crackers are just beginning to brown on the edges. Flip them all over and bake for another 5 to 10 minutes, or until they are brown on the edges and as crunchy as you prefer. If you want them crunchier, bake them longer. Note: they burn quick, so keep an eye on them if you're keeping them in longer!

Let them cool for 10 minutes, and then enjoy! These will keep at room temperature or in the fridge for 1 to 2 weeks.

Raw Option: Same instructions, but "bake" in your dehydrator at 115°F (46°C) until they're crunchy; it will take several hours.

SOY-FREE **RAW OPTION** **QUICK TO MAKE**

SEEDY HERBY CRACKERS

Hemp and flax are incredibly nutritious little seeds. These crackers offer a delicious, crunchy way to incorporate them into your diet. I like eating these with Cashew Cheese (page 227), Hummus (page 254) or crumbled on top of any savory main meal or salad. This recipe is used on page 147.

MAKES ~35 BITE-SIZE CRACKERS

¼ cup (40 g) white sesame seeds

¼ cup (40 g) black sesame seeds

¼ cup (40 g) hemp seeds

¼ cup (40 g) flax seeds

⅓ cup (37 g) ground flax seeds

½ tsp garlic powder

Salt and pepper, as desired

1–2 tbsp (2–4 g) herbes de provence, as desired

½ cup (48 g) almond flour, or almond pulp (leftover from Almond-Brazil Nut Milk, page 210)

1 tbsp (15 ml) extra-virgin olive oil

½ cup (120 ml) water, or more as needed

Preheat the oven to 350°F (177°C).

Mix all the dry ingredients together evenly, adding salt and pepper and herbes de provence to taste.

Add the olive oil and water and incorporate evenly. You should end up with a moist dough that is almost like a chunky paste. If your mixture is too crumbly, add water as needed. If it's too wet, add extra almond flour or seeds.

Line a baking sheet with parchment paper, scoop on your dough, then place another piece of parchment on top. Roll the dough out evenly between the two pieces of parchment until it's around 1 inch (2.5 cm) thick. Take off the top piece of parchment.

Score with a knife or pizza cutter into whatever sizes and shapes you desire; just make sure they're all relatively similar.

Bake for 15 minutes, and then flip them all over and bake for another 5 to 10 minutes, or until they are as crunchy as you prefer. Keep an eye on 'em!

Let them cool for 10 minutes, and then enjoy. These will keep at room temperature or in the fridge for a week.

Raw Option: Same instructions, but "bake" them in your dehydrator until crunchy; it will take several hours.

SPICED CHICKPEAS

I love this as a snack on its own or sprinkled on any savory dish. Thanks to the protein and fiber in legumes, it's quite filling. This recipe is used for Quick Broccoli Spinach Soup (page 84), Big Ole Salad (page 91) and Roasted Potatoes (page 111).

MAKES ~2 CUPS (330 G)

1 tbsp (15 ml) extra-virgin olive oil

1–2 tsp (7–14 g) ras el hanout powder, as desired

¼ tsp lemongrass powder

2 cups (330 g) cooked chickpeas

Salt and pepper, as desired

Heat the olive oil with the spices in a pan on medium-low heat.

Add the chickpeas and stir into the oil and spices until evenly coated. Add salt and pepper, if you like.

Cook for 5 minutes, stirring occasionally, until the chickpeas are beginning to smell fragrant and the spices on the chickpeas begin to brown.

Best eaten fresh!

PEANUT SAUCE WITH GINGER + CAYENNE

I will search for whatever edible things are nearest to me simply to have something to eat this sauce with. Amazing as a dip with rice paper wraps, on noodles, or drizzled over steamed or baked vegetables—especially greens. This recipe is used for a sauce on the Navy Bean Burgers (page 107).

MAKES ~2 CUPS (490 G)

½ cup (90 g) peanut butter

½ cup (120 ml) coconut milk, or more as needed

2 tbsp (30 ml) tamari

1 tbsp (15 ml) apple cider vinegar

1 tbsp (15 ml) sesame oil

½ tsp garlic powder

½ tsp cayenne powder

½ tsp ginger powder

2 pitted dates

Blend all the ingredients until smooth, adjusting to taste and adding coconut milk as needed to get the consistency you desire.

Store refrigerated for up to 2 weeks; it will thicken as time goes on. If you'd like to thin it out again, add more water and then spices, according to taste.

SOY-FREE   RAW   QUICK TO MAKE

ROSEMARY GARLIC ALMOND CREAM

Garlic and rosemary are best buds. Here they pair with creamy almonds to create a rich, savory sauce that you can use as a dressing or a drizzle, as you see fit. This cream is wonderful spread on fresh bread or combined with pasta and roasted vegetables. Optional: soak the almonds for 8 hours before using them in this recipe. This will change the texture so it's not quite as smooth, but the flavor is just as delicious and the nutrients in the almonds are more readily absorbed by your digestive system. This recipe is used with Black Bean Meatballs with Spaghetti (page 99).

MAKES ~2 CUPS (475 ML)

1 cup (170 g) almonds

1 tsp garlic powder

1 tsp dried rosemary leaves

2 tbsp (30 ml) apple cider vinegar

1 tsp brown rice syrup

¾ cup (180 ml) water, or more as needed

Salt and pepper, as desired

Blend all the ingredients until smooth, adjusting to taste and adding water as needed to get the consistency you desire.

Store refrigerated for up to 2 weeks; it will thicken as time goes on. If you'd like it to thin it out again, just add more water and then salt according to taste.

WALNUT TURMERIC SAUCE

Turmeric is a gem of a food in color, flavor and health-promoting properties. With regular consumption, this is a plant that may play a role in preventing disease such as cancer and heart attacks, reducing cholesterol and protecting brain health. Turmeric has anti-inflammatory effects on the digestive system. It can be purchased in capsule form—sometimes labelled "curcumin," which is the compound in turmeric that gives it its color and has all the health benefits we want—but making it into a comforting drink is way more fun. Consuming turmeric with black pepper increases bioavailability because of how the piperine (found in black pepper) works with the curcumin (in turmeric). This recipe is used with Roasted Potatoes with Garlic, Rosemary + Thyme on page 111.

MAKES ~2 CUPS (490 G)

1 cup (120 g) walnuts

2 tsp (6 g) turmeric powder, as desired

¼ tsp smoked paprika powder

¼ tsp cinnamon powder

¼ tsp ginger powder

¼ tsp cumin powder

¼ tsp black pepper

3 tbsp (45 ml) lime juice

1 tbsp (15 ml) tamari

1 tsp brown rice syrup

¾ cup (180 ml) water, or more as needed

Sea salt, as desired

Blend all the ingredients until smooth, adjusting to taste and adding water as needed to get the consistency you desire.

Store refrigerated for up to 2 weeks; it will thicken as time goes on. If you'd like to thin it out again, simply add more water and then salt and spices as desired.

*See photo on page 237.

NUT-FREE   **SOY-FREE**   **QUICK TO MAKE**

MAPLE DIJON DRESSING

This one's my riff on honey mustard sauce. I love the tangy balanced with the sweet here. This recipe is used in Quinoa Squash Cakes (page 95), and is great with any breaded veggies or vegan proteins.

MAKES ~¾ CUP (180 ML)

¼ cup (60 ml) maple syrup, or more as needed

⅓ cup (80 ml) Dijon mustard

½ tsp garlic powder

2 tbsp (30 ml) lemon juice

2 tbsp (10 g) nutritional yeast

2 tbsp (30 ml) extra-virgin olive oil

2 tbsp (30 ml) water, or more as needed

Salt and pepper, as desired

Blend all the ingredients together until smooth, adjusting to taste and adding water as needed to get the consistency you desire. If it's too bitter, add more maple syrup or blend in some dates.

Store refrigerated for up to 2 weeks; it will thicken as time goes on. If you'd like it to thin out again, add more water and then salt as desired.

*See photo on page 237.

SOY-FREE **RAW** **QUICK TO MAKE**

CHIPOTLE CASHEW MAYO

So creamy, so smoky, so hard to stop eating. This is great with everything: pasta, veggies, crackers, chips, BBQ, salad. . . . Can I just date chipotle? This recipe is paired with Roasted Potatoes on page 111.

MAKES ~2 CUPS (475 ML)

1 cup (110 g) cashews

3 tbsp (45 ml) lime juice

1 tsp garlic powder

¼ tsp smoked paprika powder

½ tsp chipotle powder

¾ cup (180 ml) water, or more as needed

Salt and pepper, as desired

Blend all the ingredients until smooth, adjusting to taste and adding water as needed to get the consistency you desire.

Store refrigerated for up to 2 weeks; it will thicken as time goes on. If you'd like to thin it out again, simply add more water and salt and spices as desired.

*See photo on page 237.

NUT-FREE

SOY-FREE

RAW

QUICK
TO MAKE

LEMON TAHINI POPPY SEED DRESSING

Poppy seeds are actually really nutritious (high in calcium, iron, fiber, healthy fats and B vitamins), and add a nice crunch to this creamy, zesty sauce. This recipe is used in the Big Ole Salad on page 91.

MAKES ~1 CUP (240 ML)

¼ cup (60 ml) lemon juice

⅓ cup (60 g) tahini

2 tbsp (17 g) poppy seeds

1 tsp garlic powder (optional)

⅓ cup (80 ml) water, or more as needed

Salt and pepper, as desired

Blend all the ingredients together until smooth, adjusting to taste and adding water as needed to get the consistency you desire.

Store refrigerated for up to 2 weeks; it will thicken as time goes on. If you'd like it to thin out again, simply add more water and then salt as desired.

*See photo on page 237.

NUT-FREE **QUICK TO MAKE**

SMOKED PAPRIKA BARBECUE SAUCE

This is zingy! It's a perfect marinade for tofu steaks and grilled vegetables, as a spread on epic sandwiches or in lasagna, and wonderful stirred into mac and cheese. This recipe is served with Roasted Potatoes with Garlic on page 111.

MAKES ~2 CUPS (480 ML)

⅔ cup (170 g) tomato paste

¼ cup (60 ml) tamari

2 tbsp (30 ml) apple cider vinegar

¼ cup (60 ml) maple syrup

1 tbsp (15 ml) blackstrap molasses

1 tsp garlic powder

½ tsp chipotle powder

½ tsp smoked paprika powder

2 pitted dates

⅓ cup (80 ml) water, or more as needed

Salt, as desired

Blend all the ingredients until smooth, adjusting to taste and adding water as needed to get the consistency you desire.

Store refrigerated for up to a month; it will thicken as time goes on. If you'd like it to thin out again, simply add more water and then salt as desired.

GARLIC BUTTERY SPREAD

I adore this recipe, and use it on everything from avocado toast to warm pasta to baked or steamed vegetables. It's wonderfully creamy and flavorful, and full of healthy fats thanks to hemp, coconut and olive. Feel free to add other spices like onion powder, dried thyme or rosemary.

MAKES ~1 CUP (240 ML)

¼ cup (60 ml) melted coconut oil

¼ cup (60 ml) extra-virgin olive oil

¼ cup (40 g) hemp seeds

1 tbsp (8 g) garlic powder

Extra spices and herbs (optional)

Salt and pepper, as desired

Water, as needed

Blend all the ingredients together until smooth, adjusting to taste and adding water as needed to get the consistency you desire.

Store refrigerated for up to 2 months.

ROSEMARY + THYME GRAVY

Woooow. Prepare to take your holiday meal to the next level. Or any meal, for that matter, because gravy deserves our love more than once or twice a year. This recipe is ideal smothered on roasts, as a dip for toasty bread or added into shepherd's pie; I use it in a stir-fry on page 87.

MAKES ~2 CUPS (480 ML)

1 tbsp (15 ml) extra-virgin olive oil

1 yellow onion

3 cloves garlic

1¼ cups (300 ml) mushroom broth, or vegetable broth, or more as needed

¼ cup (60 ml) tamari

1 tbsp (15 ml) apple cider vinegar

1 tbsp (15 ml) brown rice syrup

2 tsp (5 g) dried rosemary

1 tsp ground coriander

4 cloves

1 tsp garlic powder

1 tsp dried thyme

½ tsp fennel seeds

½ cup (120 ml) nondairy milk (page 209), as needed

3 tbsp (45 g) tahini

Salt and pepper, as desired

Heat the oil in a heavy-bottomed pan on medium-low heat.

Peel and mince the onion and garlic; then add them to the pan and sauté for 5 minutes or until they're translucent and beginning to brown.

Add the rest of the ingredients, and simmer for 10 to 15 minutes, or until very fragrant and thickened. If it becomes too thick, add more broth or milk.

You can leave it chunky as is, or blend until smooth. Adjust according to taste and texture.

Store in the fridge and enjoy within 2 weeks.

SOY-FREE   RAW   QUICK TO MAKE

WALNUT CILANTRO PESTO

This is my reimagining of a traditional pesto. Instead of basil, olive oil and pine nuts, we're using cilantro, walnut oil and walnuts. I prefer using garlic powder instead of raw garlic because the latter gives me a headache and leaves that familiar, very strong flavor in my mouth all day. If you'd like an alternative to Parmesan cheese, throw in a little nutritional yeast. Perfect with Pasta with Walnut Cilantro Pesto + Avocado (page 92), Garden Lasagna (page 103), as a dip or spread for crackers or raw veggies or served with baked vegetables.

MAKES ~1½ CUPS (330 G)

1 cup (120 g) walnuts

2 cups (80 g) spinach

2 cups (80 g) cilantro

¼ cup (60 ml) walnut oil

2 tbsp (30 ml) lemon juice

1 tsp garlic powder

Salt and pepper, as desired

2 tbsp (10 g) nutritional yeast (optional)

Throw all the ingredients into a food processor and process until you have a chunky paste, or continue processing if you'd like a smoother pesto.

Adjust according to taste, adding salt and pepper as desired. If you'd like it to be a bit cheesy, add nutritional yeast.

Store in the fridge for up to a week.

NUT-FREE　　**RAW**　　**QUICK TO MAKE**

GINGER SESAME DRESSING

Zesty, light and fresh. I love this as a marinade for tofu rice noodle dishes, big salads and drizzled over rice bowls. If you'd like it a bit richer and creamier, add a couple tablespoons (30 g) of tahini. This recipe is used as a dressing for the Crunchy Salad on page 112.

MAKES ~½ CUP (120 ML)

2 tbsp (29 g) minced ginger
1 tbsp (15 ml) sesame oil
1 tbsp (15 ml) lemon juice
1 tbsp (15 ml) brown rice syrup
1 tbsp (16 g) miso paste
¼ cup (60 ml) water
½ tsp garlic powder
½ tsp cayenne powder
½ tsp chia seeds
1 tsp tamari
1–2 tbsp (15–30 g) tahini (optional)
Salt and pepper, as desired

Blend or whisk all the ingredients into a dressing.

Store in the fridge and enjoy within 2 weeks.

NUT-FREE   RAW   QUICK TO MAKE

SIMPLE MISO GRAVY

The sweetness of miso, creamy nuttiness of tahini, smokiness of paprika and light tartness of lemon all work as perfect teammates here. A go-to sauce for me. This recipe is used as a spread on page 108 with sourdough bread, pesto and creamy eggplant.

MAKES ~½ CUP (110 G)

⅓ cup (80 ml) water, or more as needed

3 tbsp (35 g) tahini

1 tbsp (16 g) miso paste

1 tbsp (15 ml) lemon juice

½ tsp garlic powder

¼ tsp smoked paprika powder

Blend or whisk together all the ingredients until smooth. Adjust according to taste, adding anything else you like. Store this in the fridge for up to a week.

*See photo on page 250.

SOY-FREE   RAW   QUICK TO MAKE

HORSERADISH DRESSING

This recipe is used with Green Pea Patties on page 96, and works as a dip for veggies or fries, or a sauce for any savory meal that would pair well with a zingy flavor component.

MAKES ~1½ CUPS (360 ML)

1 cup (110 g) cashews

½ cup (120 ml) water, or more as needed

¼ cup (60 ml) extra-virgin olive oil

1–2 tbsp (15–30 g) grated horseradish, as desired

1 tsp mustard

1 tsp apple cider vinegar

1 tsp maple syrup

Salt and pepper, as desired

Blend together all the ingredients until smooth. Adjust according to taste, adding anything else you like. Store in the fridge for up to a week.

*See photo on page 250.

HUMMUS WITH CUMIN + PAPRIKA

Obviously, there's gotta be a recipe for hummus in a vegan cookbook; it's the official symbol of plant-munchers worldwide. The origins of this popular chickpea and tahini spread (also called *hummus bi tahini*, or *ummu bi aīna*) are in the Middle East and Mediterranean, where it's eaten with flatbread and/or as part of a mezze board. The best thing about this hummus recipe is the smoothness and simple, elegant flavor. It's inspired by one I have made time and time again, from *The Blossom Cookbook* by Ronen Seri and Pamela Elizabeth. This recipe is used for the Hummus 'N' Veg Board on page 151.

SERVES 5 TO 6

2¼ cups (370 g) cooked chickpeas

⅔ cup (160 ml) extra-virgin olive oil

⅓ cup (60 g) tahini

½ cup (120 ml) water, or more as needed

Scant ¼ cup (60 ml) lemon juice

1½ tsp (4 g) cumin powder

1 tsp garlic powder

¼ tsp smoked paprika powder

Salt and pepper, as desired

Blend all the ingredients until very smooth: the longer you blend, the smoother it will be. Give your blender or food processor breaks if necessary. If the hummus is too thick for your appliance, add more water and adjust the spices accordingly.

Garnish with extra olive oil on top, a sprinkling of extra chickpeas and herbs and spices (like pine nuts, cilantro, turmeric or paprika) if desired.

This will keep for up to a week in the fridge.

NUT-FREE **SOY-FREE** **RAW** **QUICK TO MAKE**

ADAPTOGENIC CHOCOLATE MIX

Blend with your fave nondairy milk for an instant mug of good feels. Recipe idea on page 64.

SERVES ~30; MAKES 4 CUPS (460 G)

1 cup (120 g) cacao powder

¾ cup (143 g) coconut sugar

⅓ cup (40 g) maca powder

⅓ cup (40 g) lucuma powder

¼ cup (30 g) reishi mushroom powder

¼ cup (30 g) chaga mushroom powder

¼ cup (30 g) ashwagandha powder

¼ cup (30 g) astragalus powder

½ tsp sea salt

½ tsp vanilla powder

⅛ tsp stevia powder

Blend all the ingredients together evenly until finely ground.

Store in a jar in the fridge or a cupboard for up to 3 months.

NUT-FREE **SOY-FREE** **RAW** **QUICK TO MAKE**

TURMERIC SPICE MIX

Blend this with coconut milk or other nondairy milk for a super quick and easy golden tonic. Recipe idea on page 67. Inspired by the popular Ayurvedic Indian drink, *haldi doodh*.

**SERVES ~20; MAKES
2 CUPS (280 G)**

¾ cup (105 g) turmeric powder

¾ cup (143 g) coconut sugar

2 tbsp (15 g) ginger powder

2 tbsp (15 g) cinnamon powder

1 tsp black pepper

¼ tsp stevia powder

⅛ tsp sea salt

Blend all the ingredients together evenly until finely ground.

Store in a jar in the fridge or a cupboard for up to 3 months.

NUT-FREE   **SOY-FREE**   **RAW**   **QUICK TO MAKE**

GREEN POWER MIX

For days I don't wanna put together a fancy salad or cook green veggies, this mix comes in handy. Fruity flavors from lucuma and baobab help balance the bitterness of the greens. I usually blend this with a banana some spinach, lemon juice and water or nondairy milk. Recipe idea on page 68.

**SERVES ~25; MAKES
3½ CUPS (405 G)**

¾ cup (143 g) coconut sugar

½ cup (60 g) lucuma powder

½ cup (60 g) baobab powder

⅓ cup (40 g) spirulina powder

¼ cup (30 g) moringa powder

¼ cup (30 g) chlorella powder

¼ cup (30 g) matcha powder

¼ cup (30 g) wheatgrass juice powder

1 tbsp (8 g) ginger powder

¼ tsp stevia powder

Blend all the ingredients together evenly until finely ground.

Store this in a jar in the fridge or a cupboard for up to 3 months.

THE SUPERFOODS

The foods that follow are known to have powerful effects on the human body: they can prevent cancer, enhance brain functionality, fight depression and anxiety, improve mood, reduce inflammation and much more. These ingredients have been proven in scientific research to have substantial health benefits. (Of course, food science has its own political complications, but that's for another book.) I have personally found that regularly consuming these foods has changed my life for the better: I think more clearly, sleep more soundly, feel more positive and creative, and recover faster from injury, temporary illness and exercise when they're in my diet.

Many of these foods have been used by cultures around the globe for generations, and so I trust that they have special healing and protective properties. In particular, the wise, rich histories of Traditional Chinese Medicine and Ayurveda in India, date back millennia and provide us with time-tested herbs, formulas and philosophies that continue to effectively treat bodies, spirits and minds today. I acknowledge and give thanks to the peoples, cultures and geographies this knowledge comes from, and I am grateful for the privilege to have access to it. If you are able, researching the histories of these ingredients is a rewarding, necessary experience that enhances the context and meaning of the food you're consuming. I believe it is important to recognize and pay homage to the origins of these ingredients instead of divorcing them from their historic, cultural landscape and roots. Cultural appropriation and neocolonialism can occur with food consumption as well as other aspects of culture, so let us be cognizant and appreciative—instead of ignorant—of where, when and who the foods we value come from. Food is not merely about nutrients: it is the story of who we are.

AMLA: Also known as Indian Gooseberry, this li'l plant is one of the richest sources of antioxidants that has been researched, according to its ORAC (Oxygen Radical Absorbance Capacity) score. An ingredient in the Ayurvedic formula Triphala, amla is high in vitamin C, can be used as a laxative and may provide neuroprotective effects. I use it in powder form; it's great in sweet fruit smoothies.

AVOCADOS: An incredible, nutritionally dense, fatty fruit boasting substantial amounts of vitamins K, C, B5, B6 and E as well as folate, potassium and fiber. The vitamins, minerals and nutrients in this green fruit can improve skin health and brain function. The fats in avocados are monounsaturated fatty acids, which may help in reducing inflammation. Fun project: you can sprout an avocado pit into a tree! Look up how to do it online.

ASHWAGANDHA: An adaptogenic herb—and member of the nightshade family—used to alleviate anxiety, stress and insomnia; reduce inflammation, blood sugar levels and cortisol; protect against cancer and strengthen the immune system. It can be a useful addition to cancer treatment. I use it in powder form: it's white and has a mild smell and taste. I love adding it to rich, warm drinks, smoothies or chocolate recipes. Ashwagandha has been utilized for over three millennia in Indian Ayurvedic medicine, so you know it works.

ASTRAGALUS: A fundamental, adaptogenic herb used in Traditional Chinese Medicine for millennia, which can protect your heart and kidneys. Astragalus has anti-inflammatory and cardioprotective properties, and can reduce cholesterol. It is believed to have longevity-promoting abilities, but these claims have not been sufficiently studied. I use astragalus in powder form and add it to drinks.

BEANS AND LENTILS (AKA LEGUMES): These babies have a ton of protein, fiber, iron, folate, magnesium and potassium, as well as smaller amounts of other vitamins and minerals. They are filling, versatile in recipes and a smart addition to most diets. The health benefits of eating legumes includes reducing cholesterol, improving blood pressure and lowering the risk of heart disease. I use beans (mostly lentils, black beans and chickpeas) in everything from brownies to savory patties to nondairy cheeses. Do not consume them raw, however, as they contain anti-nutrients in their uncooked form.

BEETS: A beautifully vibrant root vegetable packed with vitamins and minerals (including folate and manganese), and nitrates (which are known to lower blood pressure). An interesting benefit to eating beets is that they improve how your body uses oxygen, so these bright root veggies are great for athletes or people who like to workout. Eat 'em a few hours before exercise. Beet juice is a gorgeous color, too!

BLACKSTRAP MOLASSES: This thick, dark syrup is a byproduct of the cane sugar–refining process. It boasts serious amounts of calcium, potassium and iron, which are all important for blood and bone health. I would recommend adding it to smoothies and baked goods that include cinnamon, ginger and nutmeg, because then it'll taste like spiced pie or gingerbread cookies (the flavor is a little strong on its own).

CRUCIFEROUS VEGETABLES: Including cabbage, collard greens, Brussels sprouts, cauliflower, bok choy, broccoli, rutabaga, arugula and kale. These are some of the healthiest food on EARTH. These guys boast a huge amount of vitamins K and C, fiber and iron, which are important for maintaining bone, muscle and blood health. Cruciferous veggies contain antioxidants (which protect against free radical damage) and eating them regularly may reduce inflammation and strengthen immunity. Thanks to their insoluble fiber content, cruciferous vegetables help with gut health and digestion. Rutabaga specifically has antifungal properties. Tips: 1) There's nothing wrong with green cabbage, but red cabbage contains more antioxidants. 2) Eating raw cruciferous veggies may cause bloating or gas (believe me, I know), plus gently steaming some of them unlocks more nutrition anyway.

CACAO: Chocolate time! Cacao and cocoa come from the cacao plant. Cocoa is processed at higher temperatures, which takes away some of its antioxidant content and changes the flavor to a more robust, roasted and rich taste. Cacao, on the other hand, has a sharper, spicier, floral flavor profile and more antioxidants (including polyphenols). They both contain substantial amounts of fiber, zinc, iron, magnesium, copper, manganese and a decent amount of protein as well. I use cacao nibs, cacao powder and cocoa powder at home, as well as cacao and cocoa butter. I love it all.

CAMU CAMU: A tart berry, native to rainforests in Brazil and Peru, that's super rich in vitamin C, manganese and antioxidants (including caternoids). I use it in powder form and add it to smoothies to keep my immune system happy. One teaspoon of camu camu powder has about 1000% of your recommended daily intake for vitamin C. Yep.

CINNAMON: This spice is on basically everyone's 'Healthiest Foods' lists, and with good reason. It's been used for thousands of years as medicine, perhaps beginning with Egyptians in 2,000 BCE. The compound cinnamaldehyde in cinnamon is what provides many of its health advantages. It is rich in antioxidants (like polyphenols) and may protect against cancer, reduce risk for heart disease, provide anti-inflammatory properties and fight infections. Besides, it tastes delicious. Note: try to buy Ceylon cinnamon, it's the good stuff.

COCONUT: This is a wonder food and I use it in all parts of my life (including as a skin and hair moisturizer). Coconut oil is antibacterial and antimicrobial. It can balance blood cholesterol levels and boost brain function. Make sure to get extra-virgin coconut oil, as it retains way more antioxidants compared to the refined version. I cook with it, add it to raw desserts and rich, sweet drinks like hot chocolate. Dried coconut flesh, coconut butter and coconut milk most likely have benefits similar to coconut oil since they contain it, albeit in less concentrated amounts. Coconut sugar is one of my favorite sweeteners because of its amazing flavor.

DATES: The fruit of the date palm, dates are usually sold semi-dried, so they retain some moisture and gooeyness. They are super sweet and delicious with just a spoonful of nut butter, making a great energy-boosting snack when you don't feel like eating a whole meal but need some extra calories. They contain a good amount of potassium, fiber, vitamin B6, polyphenols and niacin. Considering their nutritional profile and their yummy taste, dates are one of my fave sweeteners. I blend them into all kinds of recipes, from sweet drinks to savory sauces and baked goods to salads.

EXTRA-VIRGIN OLIVE OIL: Here's an ingredient that is rich in monounsaturated oleic fat (the kind that can help seriously reduce inflammation and may play a role in fighting cancer), and antioxidants (which help protect against heart disease). Plus, it's antibacterial and can protect against infections. Just make sure you buy extra-virgin olive oil, preferably stored in a dark glass bottle. I use olive oil for cooking, moisturizing my skin and occasionally I add it to baked goods.

FENNEL SEEDS: I love fennel for two reasons. 1) Fennel extract is very effective at alleviating menstrual cramps. As in, more effective than pharmaceuticals. Mic drop. 2) When I make rice in my rice cooker, I toss a tablespoon (8 g) of fennel in with the water and uncooked rice grains, and let it all cook. When it's ready, the fennel has imparted a lovely flavor and—I swear!—makes my rice fluffier.

FRUITS: Including berries, pineapples, mangoes, peaches, pears, apples, kiwi, oranges, papaya, grapes, apples, pears, pomegranates, cucumbers, bell peppers and melons. Oh, my darlings, how I adore sweet fruits. I have tattoos of figs, peaches and blackberries because I love 'em so dang much. Juicy fruits contain a lot of water, so they are naturally hydrating foods. I don't think there's any real science to this idea, but it makes me excited to know that the water in fruits is super filtered on the cellular level, into the unique matrixes and structures that make up the food. Cool, right? More seriously though: these gems contain a hefty amount of vitamin C (great for immunity and flu prevention), antioxidants (which may help protect against cancer or free radical damage) and vitamin A (skin and eye health!). Goji berries (dried) specifically offer a decent amount of protein.

GARLIC: A deliciously savory favorite for people around the world, this spicy guy can improve cardiovascular health and cholesterol levels. It may lower blood sugar and is a great source of antioxidants. I prefer using cooked garlic, or garlic powder, in my recipes because raw garlic can give me a headache and I do not enjoy the lingering, strong taste it leaves in my mouth.

GINGER: This spice is a superstar, up there with cinnamon and turmeric. It is high in gingerol, a compound with powerful anti-inflammatory and antioxidant properties. Ginger has been used for millennia in many cultures (originating in Southeast Asia, and subsequently spreading via trade to the Mediterranean) to alleviate nausea, aid digestion and prevent colds and the flu. This root can lower blood sugar levels and has anti-inflammatory properties. The most important benefit for me is ginger's ability to reduce menstrual-related pain; it's as effective as ibuprofen. I often use ginger in powder form because its benefits are more concentrated, but fresh ginger has a magical flavor and should not be ignored.

HOLY BASIL: Affectionately known as the Queen of Herbs, this adaptogenic plant can treat myriad ailments and diseases, including helping you cope with different kinds of stress. Holy Basil is antifungal, antibacterial, antiviral, anti-inflammatory and pain relieving. Additionally, it can reduce cholesterol and lower blood sugar. I enjoy it in tea as often as possible; its flavor is delicious.

KAVA: Native to the western Pacific and traditionally consumed for spiritual, mental and physical benefits in both ceremonial and casual settings, this root may help alleviate anxiety and promote a sense of euphoria and relaxation by releasing dopamine in the brain. Additional research is needed to more fully understand how this food interacts with the human body, but it appears to be safe to consume for most folks. It might make you a little drowsy if you ingest a lot, so stay away from operating heavy machinery afterwards. I consume it in low doses (around 1 teaspoon) in powder form and make tea with it.

KIMCHI: Fermented foods, hello! Kimchi, a staple Korean side dish, and other fermented foods are rich in probiotics, which are beneficial to gut health and digestion. And of course, gut health and digestion are major players in your overall health (like everything from your skin to how well you sleep). Plus, kimchi includes cabbage, chili, ginger and garlic, which all offer health benefits in their own right. I throw kimchi on savory dinner bowls, add it to rice and sometimes blend it into curry sauces.

LEMONS AND LIMES: These juicy fruits are known for their sourness, and fresh fragrance and taste, but they provide a lot more! Lemons and limes are antiviral, high in vitamin C and strengthening for your blood vessels. I add a couple tablespoons (30 ml) of lemon or lime juice to a glass of warm water in the mornings, and you'll find me adding lime and lemon juice to all kinds of recipes every day. I love the flavor and freshness these add to food and drinks.

MACA: I use this Peruvian cruciferous root in the form of powder, and add it to chocolate and drinks. I already love maca for its flavor and adaptogenic properties; but upon researching for this book I've learned it's an excellent source of vitamin C and copper. It also has decent amounts of iron, potassium, vitamin B6 and manganese. Maca may have the ability to improve your mood and brain function as well as alleviate symptoms of menopause. That being said, more scientific studies on maca need to be done to better prove its benefits.

MUCUNA PRURIENS: Also called The Velvet Bean, this legume—especially its seeds—is used in Ayurvedic practice to help treat Parkinson's Disease and may have neuroprotective properties thanks to its antioxidant content. According to some claims, though more research is needed, it may work as an antidepressant, dopamine booster and aphrodisiac. I consume this in powder form.

MUSHROOMS: Including chaga, reishi and cordyceps. These fungi have been consumed for millennia and backed by Traditional Chinese Medicine for their purported medicinal properties and ability to fight cancer, strengthen the immune system and promote longevity. Cooking fresh mushrooms such as shiitake, portobello and enoki make them more nutritious. I use mushroom powders—like chaga, reishi and cordyceps—in hot, creamy drinks paired with maca, cacao, dates and coconut or almond milk. I adore my 14 Mushroom Blend powder from Harmonic Arts and have it every day. Mushrooms contain decent amounts of selenium, riboflavin and niacin. Some provide vitamin D (I use a vitamin D supplement extracted from mushrooms).

NUTS, SEEDS AND BUTTERS: Including almonds, cashews, walnuts, Brazil nuts, hazelnuts, pecans, pine nuts, chia seeds, pumpkin seeds, hemp seeds, flax seeds, sunflower seeds and sesame seeds. These dudes are delicious sources of healthy monounsaturated fats, and provide wonderful textures and flavors to recipes. They are most nutritious consumed raw, though lightly toasting or roasting brings out more flavor. Nuts and seeds are good for the heart and may reduce the risk of heart attack or heart disease; they provide protein, vitamin E, fiber and antioxidants. Walnuts, almonds and pecans are especially nutritious. Brazil nuts specifically are an excellent source of selenium; you only need two or three to meet your day's recommendation. My fave nut and seed butters are almond, hazelnut, peanut and tahini (sesame).

OATS: All hail the humble but mighty oat! This is one of my favorite foods because I can enjoy it in so many forms: from porridge to chia pudding to oat milk to flour in brownies. It is a terrific source of protein and may help in lowering cholesterol, reducing the risk of heart disease, enhancing the immune system, fighting inflammation and stabilizing blood sugar. Oats are technically gluten-free, but most are contaminated with gluten in their processing. So if you have celiac, opt for certified gluten-free oats. I recommend plain rolled oats: they're perfect for oatmeal and chia pudding, and you can quickly turn them into fresh oat flour or milk in seconds in a blender. Oh! Plus, oatmeal baths are powerfully healing and moisturizing for the skin.

PANAX GINSENG: Also known as True ginseng, Asian ginseng, Chinese ginseng or Korean ginseng, this anti-cancer root can boost energy, cognitive function, mood and immunity. It might help some folks with alleviating PMS symptoms.

PUMPKINS, SQUASHES AND GOURDS: I am constantly in awe of the colors, sizes and shapes that these plants can come in, from vibrant oranges to deep greens; sometimes solid, sometimes marbled with white; from smooth and long to short and ribbed.

Note: Zucchini is a squash! These foods are rich in fiber, potassium, vitamin A, beta-carotene and other components which are known to benefit eye health. I absolutely love roasting squash in a little olive or coconut oil. Also, three words: Luscious Pumpkin Pie (page 161).

QUINOA (AND OTHER PSEUDO-GRAINS): Technically this is a seed, but everyone thinks it's a grain so I am giving it its own special category apart from nuts and seeds. Quinoa has good amounts of iron, fiber and protein. It is quick to cook, and versatile in both sweet and savory dishes. You can also grind it into raw flour and use it whole, raw, ground or cooked in baked goods.

SCHISANDRA: A tart berry native to eastern Asia, Schisandra contains lignans, which are helpful in protecting against and treating neurodegenerative diseases, as well as improving cognitive function. This berry has been used for these reasons in Korean, Japanese and Chinese medicine for thousands of years, and scientific studies today show promising, corresponding results. I use the dried berries and infuse them into tea, or grind them into powder and add to blended drinks.

SPINACH: This food has all the benefits associated with other green, leafy vegetables: it provides vitamins K, A and C, iron, folate, insoluble fiber (good for digestion!), health-promoting compounds and calcium. It is often called one of the healthiest foods on the planet, because calorie for calorie, it provides a staggering amount of things that make our bodies happy. Consuming spinach can benefit eye health, play a part in preventing cancer and reduce blood pressure.

SPICES: This category is awkward because it overlaps with others a bit, so the Virgo in me is not pleased, but I'll go ahead and list my fave spices anyway. I love smoked paprika, chipotle, black pepper, cinnamon, turmeric, cayenne, ginger, rosemary, basil, garlic, cumin, coriander (cilantro), oregano, thyme, cloves, nutmeg, vanilla and cardamom. These provide impressive levels of antioxidants and, most importantly, unbeatable flavor. I use them every day.

SPIRULINA & CHLORELLA: These algaes are powerful foods. They contain chlorophyll, which can help to protect against radiation from the sun and chemotherapy treatment. They help with the removal of heavy metals from your blood. Spirulina and chlorella can improve immunity, reduce inflammation, strengthen resistance to infections, promote digestion, a healthy gut and boost metabolism. I use them in powder forms: spirulina specifically is a wonderful dark, rich green that makes my smoothies look otherworldly. It is neuroprotective. I often will just add a teaspoon to a glass of water, shake it up and drink.

SWEET POTATOES: I like Japanese sweet potatoes, white-fleshed sweet potatoes and orange-fleshed sweet potatoes the most. There are many varieties, but in North America, it seems orange-fleshed sweet potatoes are the most commonly available in grocery stores. They are rich in fiber, beta-carotene, vitamin A, potassium and provide a little calcium. They have anti-cancer, and anti-inflammatory properties.

Note: What you might think of as a yam—orange flesh, orange skin—is in fact a sweet potato. True yams look quite different (Google it!) and are not usually sold in most conventional North American stores. One of my all-time favorite foods is the simple baked sweet potato. I either do it up savory (salt, pepper, tahini and lemon juice), or sweet (cinnamon, almond butter and maple syrup).

TEA: I try to drink at least a cup of green or herbal tea every day because so much science supports its health benefits; and those benefits are big. Tea is rich in polyphenols, which are antioxidants that have anti-cancer properties. Tea is good for your heart, blood and blood vessels. It can lower cholesterol and decrease the risk of coronary artery disease. I love green, black and white tea in the mornings (they contain caffeine), and herbal teas all day long. Exploring the world of tea is a joy. There are thousands of years of cultural histories surrounding it (so many books!) and countless varieties to help with everything from energy to relaxation, and PMS to depression. Plus, it's just delicious on its own or with a splash of nondairy milk and a teaspoon of fruit-infused syrup.

TOCOTRIENOLS: Also known as rice bran solubles or tocos, this food can protect our DNA (potentially against degenerative diseases such as Alzheimer's), improve cognitive function and prevent oxidative strength. Tocos are anti-inflammatory and may prevent bone damage. They're wonderful stirred into oatmeal thanks to their nutty flavor and fluffy texture.

TOMATOES: Each summer at the farmers' market, I literally stop and drop my jaw at the vibrant bounty of organic, locally-grown tomatoes showing themselves on the tables. I cannot *believe* the rainbow of colors and shapes tomatoes can be: from deep purple to glowing yellow; tiny as a grape to bigger than my hand. Good tomatoes are heavenly simply chopped and drizzled with extra-virgin olive oil and some good flaked salt. I eat them in a lot of other ways too; they're perfect in stir-fries, sliced on raw and cooked dishes, thrown on salads, lightly cooked with olive oil, blended into rich pasta sauce or roasted with garlic in the oven. Thanks to their lycopene content, tomatoes may prevent prostate cancer (especially when lightly cooked and paired with fats like olive oil or avocados) . . . so people with a prostate: eat up! They also contain a bit of fiber, vitamin C, folate, vitamin K and potassium.

TRIPHALA: Long-used in Ayurvedic traditional medicine as a holistic treatment for the body, this herbal formulation is made up of three berry powders: Amla, Haritaki and Bibhitaki. It is high in vitamin C, can help with constipation and inflammation, reduce cholesterol and protect against cancer (since the berries are rich in polyphenols).

TURMERIC: This spice has myriad health benefits, and those benefits are best absorbed by your body when you eat turmeric with black pepper. This is because the piperine in black pepper increases absorption of curcumin by up to 2000%. Curcumin is the stuff we want in turmeric: it is a compound that has serious anti-inflammatory and antioxidant properties. It may help with brain functionality and lowering the risk of developing brain disease and heart disease. It may have the ability to fight cancer and alleviate depression. It also helps with arthritis thanks to its anti-inflammatory effects. This is one of the most powerful superfoods out there. Turmeric has benefits in both its raw and cooked forms, so enjoy both. Its nutrition is concentrated in powder form.

YOGURT: This fermented, creamy treat is wonderful paired with berries, chopped nuts and a drizzle of maple syrup. It is a probiotic food, which benefits digestive health, and it contains a respectable amount of protein and calcium. I love thick, nondairy yogurts made from coconut the most, but almond and cashew varieties can be yummy too. It really depends on the brand, though. I favor a locally made, almond-based yogurt most of the time.

PANTRY LIST

The list of superfoods (page 263) doubles as a guide to what I'd recommend you keep in your kitchen or pantry. Along with those foods, I would suggest you have tamari, maple syrup or brown rice syrup, rice vinegar, nutritional yeast and some good sea salt, flaked salt or smoked salt on hand. These ingredients add a lot of flavor to recipes, and I use them often.

STORAGE & PREPARATION

Many of the ingredients I talk about (like powders, nuts and seeds) are fine to leave in your pantry or a cool, dark place for up to several months. However, when it's an option I prefer to store most of these in the fridge or freezer anyways, to keep them as fresh as possible. Fresh fruits and veggies are best eaten as soon as possible once they're ripe. I'm a fan of prepping my ingredients in advance so they're ready to go when I am hungry. For example: when I buy a cabbage, I immediately wash and chop the entire thing and then keep it in a ziploc bag in the fridge. This makes it way more convenient—and thus appealing—for me to use. Depending on what you'll be using certain ingredients for, it might be best to buy them frozen: berries and other fruits if you like them in your smoothies, jams or blended desserts, or spinach and other veggies if you'll use them in soups or sauces. Frozen foods are picked when they are ripe, and frozen right away, so they are often more nutritious and, ironically, fresher than the fresh produce in the grocery store.

Of course, organic, locally grown and ethically harvested foods are best for our bodies, our neighbors and our planet, so do buy those if available. Farmers' markets, urban and community gardens and local food co-ops and initiatives are important to support if possible.

EQUIPMENT

I keep things pretty basic in my kitchen because I can't be bothered to wash a lot of dishes once I'm finished making food. But there are a few items you'll wanna have around to make my recipes (and most other plant-based recipes as well).

For many of the recipes in here (but not all), you're gonna need:

- **HIGH-SPEED BLENDER:** I recommend Vitamix or Blendtec. They're worth the investment. My mom bought our Vitamix 15 years ago; I use it at least twice a day and it still runs perfectly. The twister jar attachment for the Blendtex is divine for making your own flours and nut butters.
- **FOOD PROCESSOR, WITH DIFFERENT ATTACHMENTS:** I recommend KitchenAid or Cuisinart.
- **CHEESECLOTH OR A NUT MILK BAG:** if you intend to make nut milks and want them super smooth.
- **MANDOLINE:** for slicing vegetables into noodles or thin strips! You can also use a cheese grater or cheese slicer with slightly different results.
- **SHARP KNIVES:** get yourself in a knife sharpener! And a durable cutting board.
- **CHOCOLATE MOLDS:** if you wanna make chocolate! Not necessary but highly recommended.
- **OTHER KITCHEN BASICS:** like a whisk, grater, peeler, baking sheets, parchment paper, a bread pan and nonstick pans.

RECOMMENDED RESOURCES

COMPANIES

Food
- Bob's Red Mill
- Harmonic Arts
- Nuzest
- Prana

Equipment
- Blendtec (blender with Twister Jar attachment)
- Braun (MultiQuick 9 hand blender)
- Vitamix (blender)

Body care
- Luminance Skincare (soap, moisturizers, masks, toners, etc.)
- Thesis Beauty

Household cleaning
- Dr. Bronner's (soap)
- Vinegar
- Baking soda
- Lemon juice

BOOKS
- *The Color of Food* by Natasha Bowens
- *Cultivating Food Justice*, edited by Alison Hope Alkon and Julian Agyeman
- *Eating Animals* by Jonathan Safran Foer
- *Eat to Live* by Joel Fuhrman, MD
- *How Not to Die* by Michael Greger, MD, and Gene Stone
- *Intuitive Eating* by Evelyn Tribole, MS, RD, and Elyse Resch, MS, RD, FADA
- *Sistah Vegan*, edited by A. Breeze Harper and Pattrice Jones
- *Veganism in an Oppressive World*, edited by Julia Feliz Brueck

COOKBOOKS
- *Ani's Raw Food Kitchen* by Ani Phyo
- *Beautifully Real Food* by Sam Murphy
- *Bowls of Goodness* by Nina Olsson
- *15 Minute Vegan* by Katy Beskow
- *The First Mess Cookbook* by Laura Wright
- *Food 52: VEGAN* by Gena Hamshaw
- *The Greenhouse Cookbook* by Emma Knight with Hanna James, Deeva Green and Lee Reitelman
- *The Mix* by Liora Bels
- *N'Ice Cream* by Virpi Mikkonen and Tuulia Talvio
- *The New Vegan* by Áine Carlin
- *Raw Food, Real World* by Matthew Kenney and Sarma Melngailis
- *Simply Vibrant* by Anya Kassoff and Masha Davydova
- *Vegan Goodness* by Jessica Prescott
- *Vegan in 7* by Rita Serano
- *Vegan Richa's Indian Kitchen* by Richa Hingle
- *Vegan Soul Food* by Bryant Terry

DOCUMENTARIES
- Angry Inuk
- Blackfish
- Cowspiracy
- Fattitude
- Feel Rich
- Food, Inc.
- Food Chains
- *Rotten* (TV series)
- Soul Food Junkies

PODCASTS
- *Food Psych Podcast*
- *The Fat Lip*
- *The Racist Sandwich* podcast
- *Rich Roll Podcast*

PLANT-BASED BLOGS AND BLOGGERS
- Amy Chaplin
- Cashew Kitchen
- Cocoon Cooks
- Earthsprout
- Erin Ireland
- The First Mess
- Green Kitchen Stories
- The Green Life
- Jenny Mustard
- My New Roots
- Oh, Lady Cakes
- Our Food Stories
- Rachele Cateyes (@radfatvegan)
- Spice and Sprout
- Sweet Potato Soul
- Tasty as Heck
- Tending the Table
- Vegan Miam
- Vegan Richa
- Vegan Yack Attack
- The Viet Vegan
- Will Frolic for Food
- Wholehearted Eats

ORGANIZATIONS, WEBSITES AND PUBLICATIONS
- Bitch Media
- Aphro-ism
- The Body Is Not An Apology
- *Chickpea* magazine
- Everyday Feminism
- Food Empowerment Project (foodispower.org)
- Health at Every Size (HAES)
- NutritionFacts.org
- Project Intersect
- *Wear Your Voice* magazine

ACKNOWLEDGMENTS

I want to thank my amazing friends for trying all the food I threw at you over the course of writing this book. Your love and support keeps me going.

Thanks, Mom, for always giving me your brutally honest critiques of my recipes (and Dad, for just accepting whatever plate or cup I put in front of you).

Thank you to Prana, Nuzest, Eternal Abundance, Harmonic Arts and Bob's Red Mill for providing many of the necessary ingredients I experimented with for the recipes.

Thanks to Carly Mucha (@carlymucha on Instagram) for offering up your beautiful ceramics for my food styling and photography! (Other pottery featured in this book comes mostly from Amanda Marie and Sarah Kersten.)

Thanks to all the bloggers and cookbook authors who inspire me with your own food photography and recipe designs.

Finally, thanks, of course, to Page Street! Especially Meg Baskis, Meg Palmer and Marissa Giambelluca. Sorry I was a bit late with this manuscript. Life just keeps *happening*!

ABOUT THE AUTHOR

Emily von Euw is the creator of the award-winning recipe blog, This Rawsome Vegan Life, as well as the bestselling author of three cookbooks: *Rawsome Vegan Baking; 100 Best Juices, Smoothies and Healthy Snacks*; and *The Rawsome Vegan Cookbook*. Em's passion in life comes from friendships, food, forests, mountains, meadows and music. They have presented at veg expos and festivals across Canada and the US and live in the lower mainland of British Columbia, Canada, on the traditional and unceded territories of the Musqueam, Squamish, and Tsleil-Waututh First Nations. Emily is a nonbinary, genderqueer person and uses they/them pronouns.

INDEX